Orkney Island Travel guide
Tourism

Author
Kingsley Foster

Copyright Notice

Copyright © 2017 Global Print Digital
All Rights Reserved

Digital Management Copyright Notice. This Title is not in public domain, it is copyrighted to the original author, and being published by **Global Print Digital**. No other means of reproducing this title is accepted, and none of its content is editable, neither right to commercialize it is accepted, except with the consent of the author or authorized distributor. You must purchase this Title from a vendor who's right is given to sell it, other sources of purchase are not accepted, and accountable for an action against. We are happy that you understood, and being guided by these terms as you proceed. Thank you

First Printing: 2017.

ISBN: 978-1-912483-53-2

Publisher: Global Print Digital.
Arlington Row, Bibury, Cirencester GL7 5ND
Gloucester
United Kingdom.
Website: www.homeworkoffer.com

.

Table of Content

Introduction 1
History 4
   Adventurers 5
      John Rae 8
      John Gow 10
   Archaeology in Orkney 12
   Literary Figures 14
      George Mackay Brown 17
   Ness of Brodgar 19
   Orcadian People 20
   The Ba 22
Culture 25
   Agricultural Shows 25
   Museums and Galleries 27
   Music in Orkney 32
   Orkney Folk Festival 34
   Orkney Science Festival 35
   St Magnus International Festival 36
   Other Festivals in Orkney 38
Travel and Tourism 41
   Getting to Orkney 43
   Life in Orkney 45
   A Prepared Welcome 46
      Clubs in Orkney 47
      Health and Social Care 49
      Education 51
      Sport and Leisure 53
      Events in Orkney 57
      Housing in Orkney 59
      Property for Sale 61
      Shopping in Orkney 71
      Transport in Orkney 72
   Products 75
      Art in Orkney 76
      Craftmakers in Orkney 78
      Orkney's Food and Drink 79
      Jewellery in Orkney 82
      Photography in Orkney 83

Nature and Wildlife 84
Animals in Orkney 85
Birds 87
- Fulmars 88
- Guillemots 89
- Razorbills 90
- Puffins 91
- Gannets 92
- Great Skua 93
- Wading Birds 94
- Birds of Prey 96
- Sea Eagle 97
- Migrating Ducks 98

Orkney's climate 102
Coast 103
Flora 105
Sealife 107
- Porpoise 108
- Dolphins 109
- Whales 111
- Seals 112
- Basking Sharks 114

Seasons in Orkney 115
- Orkney Spring 115
- Orkney Summer 116
- Orkney Autumn 118
- Orkney Winter 120

Explore Orkney 121
Kirkwall 122
Stromness 123
East Mainland 126
West Mainland 128
Burray 130
South Ronaldsay 132
Eday 133
Flotta 135
Hoy and Graemsay 137
North Ronaldsay 138
Papa Westray 140
Rousay, Egilsay and Wyre 143
Sanday 145

Shapinsay 147
Stronsay 149
Westray 151
Investing *153*
    Business Advice in Orkney 154
    Commercial Properties in Orkney 155
    Get connected in Orkney 158
    Orkney's Economic Profile 159
    Funding and Infrastructure 161
    Orkney's Main Towns 165
        Kirkwall 165
            Kirkwall Townscape Heritage Initiative 167
        Stromness 169
    Industry sectors in Orkney 170
        Agriculture in Orkney 171
        Arts and Crafts in Orkney 173
        Construction in Orkney 174
        Energy of Orkney 175
        Fishing Industry in Orkney 178
        Orkney Food and Drink 179
        Tourism in Orkney 180

Introduction

About us

Orkney is a group of islands lying six miles off the north-east tip of Scotland, separated from the mainland by the Pentland Firth — a volatile and turbulent stretch of water where three tides collide. While this makes for some bumpy ferry crossings, it gives rise to some of the best opportunities to harness tidal energy in the world.

Iconic landmarks include the Old Man of Hoy sea stack; Neolithic village Skara Brae; standing stone circle, the Ring of Brodgar, and the splendid red and yellow sandstone medieval cathedral in Kirkwall, dedicated to martyred Norse Earl St Magnus.

Orkney is saturated with history, while embracing some of the most cutting edge and innovative cultural activity in the country. The multi-million pound, award-winning gallery in Stromness, the Pier Arts Centre, holds one of the most important permanent collections of contemporary art in the UK, including works by Barbara Hepworth and

Ben Nicholson. The midsummer celebration of the arts, the St Magnus International Festival, attracts performers and audience from all over the world, while engaging the community in all aspects of the festival, creative, technical and behind-the-scenes.

This is the tip of the iceberg. Something about Orkney attracts creative people, who tend to stay. It's hard to pinpoint exactly the combination of qualities that inspires people in the islands, but it's something to do with the landscape, the light, the wide open skies, the bird and wildlife, and the legacy of cultural excellence that has run through generations.

Orkney was always a strategic hub. Four hundred years ago it was a base for the Hudson's Bay trading company, and more recently, it was an important base for the armed forces through both world wars. In 1919, the interned German fleet was scuttled in Scapa Flow. During the Second World War, Italian prisoners-of-war, brought to Orkney to work on the Churchill barriers linking the South Isles, built a chapel from two Nissen huts. Hand painted by craftsman Domenico Chiochetti, the chapel remains as a significant monument and is still used as a place of worship and as a venue.

There have always been people coming and going in Orkney, and the resulting community is open and broad-minded, looking out to the rest of the world. Orcadians are to be found in every corner of the earth, and the community in Orkney embraces people from all parts of the world and all walks of life.

In music, art and literature, Orkney's community is second to none. Through these pages you can find links to some of the recent activity, and find out more about Orkney's unique culture and history, which makes it one of the most forward-looking and exciting group of islands in the world.

History

Orkney's History

People have called Orkney home for over 5,000 years

The name "Orkney" is thought to date back to at least the 1st Century BC. First occupied by Mesolithic and Neolithic tribes and then by the Picts, Orkney was settled by Vikings during the eighth century, becoming a Norse Earldom in the ninth. Orkney was an important seat of power in the Viking Empire, a heritage best reflected by the magnificent 12th century catherdral of St Magnus in Kirkwall and through the islands' distinctly Scandinavian place names.

The islands remained under Norse rule until 1472, when they were annexed by the Scottish Crown following the failed payment of a dowry for James III's bride, Margaret of Denmark. Strong cultural links with Norway remain to this day.

And Orkney played a strategically vital role during two world wars, with the vast natural harbour of Scapa Flow acting as naval anchorage.

You can see evidence of this all around Scapa Flow, from defences and lookouts to sunken block ships, the Churchill Barriers, the Italian Chapel (built by Italian prisoners of war) and the buoy which marks the tragic loss of the HMS Royal Oak.

In our more recent history, the islands have played a key part in the development of North Sea and Atlantic Ocean oil and gas fields and are now a global centre for marine energy developers.

Adventurers

People from Orkney have made their mark on communities and industries around the world for hundreds of years. From the cold and harsh Canadian winters, to the baking heat of Australia, there are traces of Orcadian history everywhere. Here are just some of our famous adventurers.

William Balfour Baikie

Explorer, naturalist and surgeon William Balfour Baikie was born in Kirkwall in 1825. He is remembered for opening navigation of the River Niger in Africa and establishing a market for trade. After studying medicine in Edinburgh, Baikie joined the Royal Navy as a surgeon. He took part in the Niger Expedition in 1854 and went on to found the Lokoja settlement. He was anti-slavery and known for his welfare for the people, while running the trading post. He died of malignant fever while on leave in Sierra Leone, aged just 39. You can see his stone monument in St Magnus Cathedral, Kirkwall.

Eliza Fraser

This Stromness woman who was shipwrecked on the Great Barrier Reef in 1863 is a famous figure in Australian popular culture. Eliza and her sea captain husband had set sail for Sydney but were shipwrecked. They and the crew made it to Great Sandy Island, renamed Fraser Island for Eliza. She claimed later they were abducted by native people and forced to work and her husband was killed. She was rescued by escaped convict John Graham. She became a celebrity in Australia following tales of her colourful adventures. Despite marrying another sea captain she kept this secret to claim destitution on her return to the UK. The story of this Orkney woman has inspired books, paintings and a film. There is a blue commemorative plaque on her former house in Stromness.

Margaret Graham

There is also a memorial plaque in the cathedral to Margaret Graham, a nurse and missionary who devoted her life to the children and the sick of Nigeria. She was born in Orphir, Orkney in 1860 and died in Africa in 1933.

Isabel Gunn

Many Orkney men joined the Hudson's Bay Company to earn a decent wage and work in the harsh conditions of Canada, but white women were excluded in the early 19th century. Brave Isabel Gunn was driven by poverty, or some say love, to disguise herself as a man, signing on in 1806 as John Fubbister, her father's name. The 'lad' John worked well and no one suspected her secret until she gave birth to a son in the house of shocked chief factor Alexander Henry. Isabel was given work as a washerwoman in Canada but she and her son James settled in Stromness in 1809 where she lived in poverty, working as a seamstress. She died in 1861, aged 81.

Jack Renton

The amazing tales of Jack Renton, a young Orkney sailor who became a white head-hunter in the South Seas, made him a celebrity on his return to Britain. Renton told of how he was shanghaied in San Francisco in 1868 but escaped with others on a makeshift craft and washed up on Malaita in the Solomon Islands, inhabited by head-hunters and cannibals. He was sold to the chief who protected him but after eight years he escaped by sending a message on timber written with charcoal to a passing slave ship. He too was feted in Australia before returning home to Orkney. But he hankered for the South Seas and returned there, to be murdered by another tribe in the New

Hebrides. You can see a small exhibition about Renton in the Stromness Museum which includes a necklace of teeth, given to Renton as a charm.

William Tomison

He was born in 1740 in South Ronaldsay, Orkney, and aged 20 joined the Hudson's Bay Company as a labourer in the fur trade in Canada. Despite his lack of education, he rose to become Governer and Inland Chief, based in Manitoba. He founded the trading post which grew into the city of Edmonton. He retired home to Orkney, and died in 1829, leaving a bequest to found a school, Tomison's Academy. This was built in 1851 and provided free education for local children. He is buried in the garden of his former home across the road from the school.

John Rae

Dr John Rae is one of Orkney's most famous sons. An Arctic explorer, this remarkable man discovered the last navigable link in the Northwest Passage and the fate of the doomed Franklin expedition; one of the great mysteries of the Victorian age.

John Rae was born at the Hall of Clestrain in the parish of Orphir in Orkney in 1813. His Orcadian childhood spent fishing and hunting prepared him for a life of adventure and endurance. He graduated from medical school in Edinburgh and sailed from Stromness to join the Hudson's Bay Company as a doctor.

His Orcadian character helped him quickly adapt to life in the harsh Arctic conditions in Canada, learning his survival skills from native people. He went on to lead four successful expeditions charting the coast and found what would be named Rae's Strait, the last link in the Northwest Passage, in 1854. He also discovered what had happened to the 1845 lost Franklin Expedition which had attempted to find the passage. Inuit hunters told Rae that all members of the expedition were dead. Rae returned to London with the sensational evidence that the doomed naval men had been driven to cannibalism in a bid to survive. This courageous Orkney man stood by his report and evidence, despite his being damned by a shocked society. A fierce campaign was mounted against him by Lady Franklin, Sir John Franklin's widow, which was joined by Charles Dickens. Rae was deprived of a knighthood, unlike Franklin.

The Orkney doctor was, however, made a Fellow of the Royal Society in 1880. He died in 1893, aged 80, in London and his body was taken home to Orkney. He is buried in St Magnus Cathedral kirkyard in Kirkwall. Inside the cathedral you can see his magnificent stone memorial. His effigy wears Arctic clothes, his gun by his side. Calls for official recognition for the extraordinary achievements of this unsung Orkney hero have been made by survival expert Ray Mears and comedian Billy Connolly, who have both visited Orkney.

Dr John Rae, his life and legacy were the subject of a major international conference in Orkney in 2013, the bicentenary of his birth. A statue of the Arctic explorer by local sculptor Ian Scott was unveilved at the Stromness Pierhead during the event.

The John Rae Society has been launched locally to help raise awareness of the man and his achievements. You can also find out more about Dr John Rae at Stromness Museum.

John Gow

John Gow was a pirate who grew up in Orkney and was to inspire famous Scottish novelist Sir Walter Scott. Gow's trial for murder and piracy was reported by Robinson Crusoe writer Daniel Defoe.

Gow was probably born in Wick, Caithness in 1699 and moved to Stromness the following year. Legend says he ran away to sea. In 1724 he joined the ship Caroline as second mate and gunner. There was unrest on board over conditions and after two months in Santa Cruz, Tenerife, mutineers cut the throats of three officers and Gow shot the captain and threw his body overboard. Gow was elected captain of the ship, renamed Revenge, and was famed for acts of piracy in the Bay of Biscay.

In January 1725 he returned to Orkney to lie low, passing himself off as Mr Smith, a wealthy trader, and courting a local woman, Miss Helen Gordon. But, when the captain of a visiting merchant vessel recognised him, rumours of his life of crime began to circulate. Some of his crew took advantage of this to escape to the Scottish mainland, while one went to Kirkwall to warn the justices that Gow planned to attack local gentry in Orkney.

Gow and his remaining men raided the Hall of Clestrain in Orphir – home of the High Sheriff of Orkney. They sailed on to attack Carrick House in Eday but were captured when they ran aground on the Calf of Eday.

Gow was taken to London in chains to be tried at the Old Bailey. He was sentenced to death for murder and piracy. Gow had to climb the gallows twice as the rope broke during the first attempt to hang him.

Daniel Defoe's sensational account of the trial of the Orkney pirate has been reprinted a number of times, but a facsimile version taken from the original 1725 edition has been produced by Stromness Museum in a limited edition of 250. Sir Walter Scott's novel, The Pirate, is loosely based on the exploits of John Gow.

Archaeology in Orkney

You may have heard the saying that if you scratch the surface of Orkney, it bleeds archaeology.

Whilst we don't recommend digging up the landscape (unless you're an archaeologist or a farmer, of course) Orkney's rich legacy spans more than 5,500 years and we do have more ancient sites dotted around than anywhere else in Europe, with new discoveries still being made.

Indeed, the archaeological world is still abuzz over the emergence of a huge Neolithic site, possibly a temple complex, at the Ness of Brodgar, close to some of the other jewels in Orkney's archaeological crown – the Standing Stones of Stenness, the Ring of Brodgar and Maeshowe chambered tomb. All of these breathtakingly well preserved ancient treasures lie within a UNESCO World Heritage Site area, the Heart of Neolithic Orkney.

Outside the Heart of Neolithic Orkney, there are a staggering number of other major archaeological sites across Orkney. There appear to be more visible remains in Orkney's landscape than elsewhere in the UK and every year there are new finds. There are so many remains it is impossible to mention all the sites here. However, Historic Scotland, Visit Scotland and Orkney Islands Council produce material which details many of the sites of interest, as do isles publications, and there are many books detailing the county's fascinating history. Orkneyjar is a good source of information online.

The Ness of Brodgar, discovered in 2003, throws up new and exciting finds regularly during its annual dig, and its scale and sophistication suggest that Orkney may have been the cultural centre of this country thousands of years ago.

The Ness of Brodgar is usually open to visitors during the summer period that archaeologists are on site making ever more fascinating discoveries. No official tour dates have been announced for the 2016 season yet but, subject to funding, the dig season will run between the 4th of July and the 26th of August. Please be aware that the site is covered over for protection outwith the excavation weeks.

Recent discoveries at the Ness of Brodgar include the earliest known examples of grooved ware pottery and walls painted with colour. Elsewhere, the Orkney Venus, or Westray Wife, was found at the Links of Noltland in Westray. She is the oldest found representation of a human figure in Scotland. A Stone Age tomb, containing a 5000-year-old skull was discovered in a garden at Banks in South Ronaldsay in October 2010.

Archaeologists carry out annual digs in the summer at several important sites including the Links of Noltland in Westray, Rousay, Wyre and Windwick, South Ronaldsay. Marine archaeology projects investigating underwater sites are ongoing too. There are many specialists in Orkney offering commercial archaeology services and archaeology holidays and we also have the Orkney Archaeological Society, a charity which hosts regular talks.

Literary Figures

Orkney has had more than its fair share of writers, who were either born or lived in the county. Many drew on Orkney's landscape, history and people for inspiration and themes. Here, we explore some of our most famous literary figures.

Eric Linklater

Self-styled Orcadian novelist Eric Linklater (1899–1974) was born in South Wales but considered himself Orcadian. His father was a native. Linklater served in the trenches of the Somme as a sniper in World War One and narrowly escaped death when a bullet passed through his metal helmet. The helmet can be seen in the Orkney Museum in

Kirkwall. He rose to prominence as a journalist and a novelist with an international reputation. His Orcadian novels are White-maa's Saga (1929), The Men of Ness (1932) and Magnus Merriman (1934). He settled aged 35 in Harray, Orkney. His family home is now the Merkister Hotel. During World War Two he commanded Fortress Orkney. He is buried in the Harray kirkyard.

Edwin Muir

Poet, translator, prolific essayist, critic and novelist Edwin Muir (1887–1959) was born the son of a tenant farmer in Deerness in Orkney's East Mainland and spent his early years on the Orkney isle of Wyre. At the age of 14 he was uprooted to endure the culture shock of industrial Glasgow. The upheaval saw his parents and two brothers die within five years. He married Shetland-born writer Willa Anderson and the couple translated 40 novels from German and Czech, including Franz Kafka's The Trial. Muir was Director of the British Council in Prague, and later Rome. After many years travelling in Europe, in 1950 he became warden of Newbattle Abbey College in Midlothian where he encouraged fellow Orcadian writer, George Mackay Brown. Muir produced poetry from his mid-thirties, for which he was internationally acclaimed.

Robert Rendall

Robert Rendall (1898–1967) was born in Glasgow of Westray parents who moved back to Orkney when Rendall was young. He attended Kirkwall Grammar School until aged 13 and worked in the family draper shop, George Rendall. The shop was on the corner of Bridge Street and Albert Street in Kirkwall, now occupied by The Brig Larder, where a special plaque marks the building's history. Robert Rendall produced many poetry collections in the Orkney dialect and was also a keen naturalist, an expert in Orkney shells and an amateur painter. He discovered the Broch of Gurness in 1929 while sketching. His studies extended to archaeology, science, natural history and theology.

Mary Brunton

Regency novelist Mary Brunton (1778–1818) was born in Burray, Orkney, and her two complete novels propelled her into celebrity, but they are now almost forgotten. The daughter of Colonel Thomas Balfour of Elwick and Frances Ligonier, the sister of an earl, Mary eloped from the isle of Gairsay with Church of Scotland minister Alexander Brunton and settled in Edinburgh. Jane Austen branded Brunton's novel Self-Discipline as absurd. Her novels feature independent women rather than sugary heroines.

Joseph Storer Clouston

Joseph Storer Clouston (1870–1944) was a prolific author and historian whose most famous novel was The Lunatic at Large (1899). His thriller The Spy in Black was made into a film in 1930. A fellow of the Orkney Antiquarian Society, and a Fellow of the Society of Antiquaries, he also wrote A History of Orkney (1932).

Christina M Costie

Christina M Costie (1902–1967) was a Kirkwall poet whose work was penned in the Orkney dialect. Her poem Speech was a reaction to the local education director in 1952 who urged locals to abandon dialect.

George Mackay Brown

George Mackay Brown is perhaps Orkney's best known author. He was born in Stromness in 1921 and his poetry, plays, novels and short stories continue to have an impact worldwide.

A sense of place at the heart of George Mackay Brown's work brings many visitors to Orkney every year. His work was inspired by Orcadian folklore – the myths, legends and sagas - Orkney's Norse heritage, the natural landscape, his childhood and exploration of his faith. He wrote about his hometown of Stromness and chronicled the lives of the people who lived here and the way of life.

After six years as the Stromness correspondent for the Orkney Herald and a period recovering from tuberculosis, GMB, as he is often referred to in Orkney, from 1951 studied at Newbattle College in Midlothian under warden Edwin Muir, a fellow Orcadian writer. He went on to read English at Edinburgh University, returning to Orkney in 1961.

Dubbed by some as the Orkney bard, his first book of poems sold out in days. Despite almost continual ill-health he continued to write and gained numerous prizes for his work. These included the James Tait Memorial Prize for his novel The Golden Bird: Two Orkney Stories. Beside the Ocean of Time was shortlisted for the Booker Prize and won the Scottish Book of the Year title from the Saltire Society. He was awarded the OBE and three honorary degrees.

A meeting with composer Sir Peter Maxwell Davies, who has a home in Orkney, led to many collaborations between the two artists. An opera, The Martyrdom of St Magnus, was performed in 1977 at the first St Magnus Festival.

His weekly column which ran for more than 25 years in The Orcadian from 1971 is in print in book form and gives an insight into his Stromness routines and his observations on a changing Orkney.

George Mackay Brown died in 1996 but his legacy lives on in his words, and in the George Mackay Brown Fellowship.

Ness of Brodgar

The Ness of Brodgar is an archaeological site covering 2.5 hectares, sited between the Ring of Brodgar and the Standing Stones of Stenness in the Heart of Neolithic Orkney World Heritage Site.

Excavations at the site began in 2003. These have provided evidence of housing, decorated stone slabs, a massive stone wall with foundations, and a large building described as a Neolithic cathedral. The site may have been occupied from as early as 3500 BC to the close of the Neolithic period more than a millennium and a half later.

According to project manager Nick Card, of Orkney College's Institute of Archaeology, the discoveries are unparalleled in British prehistory, the complexity of finds is changing the "whole vision of what the landscape was 5,000 years ago" and "it's of a scale that almost relates to the classical period in the Mediterranean with walled enclosure and walled precincts". Additionally, according to archaeologists in general, the site could be more important than Stonehenge.

Pottery, cremated animal bones, stone tools and polished stone mace heads have been discovered and in July 2010 a rock coloured red, orange and yellow was unearthed. This was the first discovery in Britain of evidence that Neolithic peoples used paint to decorate their buildings.

A baked clay artefact known as the "Brodgar Boy", and thought to be a figurine with a head, body and two eyes, was also unearthed in the rubble of one structure in 2011.

In 2013 an intricately-inscribed stone was found, described as "potentially the finest example of Neolithic art found in the UK for several decades". A few days later archaeologists discovered a carved stone ball, a very rare find.

The site is normally only excavated for a short period during July and August and visitors are welcome to attend during that time. The 2017 excavation dates have been confirmed as Monday 3rd July until Friday 25th August. Public access and guided tours start on Wednesday 5th July until Wednesday 23rd August.

Outwith the period of the annual dig, this site is covered over to protect it from the elements and prevent deterioration, and so unfortunately there is very little to see.

Orcadian People

When local residents leave the islands, whether for a short business trip, a longer holiday or for a permanent move, the chances are they will always run into another Orcadian at some point on their journey. People from Orkney have travelled and settled across the globe for thousands of years, and it's a practice that continues to this day

Adventurers, explorers, pirates, writers and artists are among the Orcadians who have made their names around the world.

Many travelled from their native islands to make their mark on history including Arctic explorer Dr John Rae, Africa pioneer William Balfour Baikie and the more infamous pirate John Gow, immortalised by Daniel Defoe. An Orkney literary tradition was written by George Mackay Brown, Eric Linklater and others.

Orkney has punched way above its weight in inspirational people who have influenced the wider world.

James Petrie Chalmers
Orkney has its fair share of authors and other literary figures, but one local man was also hailed as a pioneer of cinema. The story of James Petrie Chalmers is one of great innovation, but unfortunately one which ended in tragic circumstances.

This pioneer of cinema was born in Tankerness in the East Mainland of Orkney in 1866, the son of a crofter. James Petrie Chalmers's working life began as an apprentice printer/compositor for the Orkney Herald newspaper in Kirkwall. As a young man he emigrated from Orkney to the USA, settling in New York. He gained a place in the history of cinema by championing the new technology of the moving image.

At a time when several companies were vying to control the fledgling film industry, Chalmers co-founded, published and edited the first independent trade paper, The Moving Picture World, in 1907. Despite pressure from some powerful companies, he continued to publish independently, highlighting all new inventions, safety standards and reviewing new films therefore allowing access to information for the whole industry.

James Petrie Chalmers died tragically aged 46, at a film convention in Dayton, Ohio, when he mistook the door of a liftshaft in a dark corridor, for that of the projection room. His funeral was attended by leading figures of the film industry and was filmed by Pathe News.

After his death his family continued to run the magazine in his memory.

The Ba

If you arrive in Kirkwall in the days or even weeks leading up to Christmas you might wonder if the town is about to be besieged.

Wooden barricades are erected to protect doors and windows as if from some sort of violent attack. The truth is that the barricades are put up to protect buildings from hundreds of bodies that surge through the streets in pursuit of a leather trophy; the Ba'.

Kirkwall's Ba' games are held on Christmas Day and New Year's Day (unless these fall on a Sunday, then it's Boxing Day and 2nd January) with both men's and boys' games played on each day. A remnant of mass football games, accounts for the Ba' begin in the 1800s, though it is believed the tradition is much older. Men of all backgrounds and ages compete for the prized leather ball. What they have in common is a huge passion for the game.

To see the action for yourself - from the safety of your computer - have a look at this short trailer, filmed in Kirkwall as part of a wider film on the history of ball games around the world.

There are two sides, the Uppies and Doonies, their names derived from Up-the-Gates or Doon-the-Gates, from Old Norse 'gata' for a road. The Ba' is thrown up to the crowd at the Mercat Cross in Kirkwall. The Uppies' goal is up the street opposite the Catholic church and the Doonies is down in the harbour - salt water must be involved for a doonie win. A Doonie was traditionally one born between the line of Old Post Office Lane and the harbour, with Uppies from the other side of the line. People born outside Orkney, say in Aberdeen, or even at Balfour Hospital on the edge of Kirkwall have been taken into town for the first time by a circuitous route to favour their family's allegiance.

The Men's Ba' is thrown up at 1pm by an honoured Ba' veteran or supporter to a crowd of up to two hundred players. The leather ball disappears into the scrum, sometimes for hours, and is keenly watched by excited spectators. There may be twists and turns as one side gains control, and there could be smuggling and fake runs up or down the street to cause confusion among the players. The game is over when the Ba' reaches the goal of one of the sides and then comes the task of the winning team deciding who is the Ba' winner. This is an honour given to a player who has played hard over several Ba' games, not a one-off man of the match award. He gets to take the Ba' home and it is traditional to throw a party open to anyone who has played.

The Boys' Ba' is played at 10am and is open to local youths under 16. While the Ba' is a male bastion nowadays, there have been two Women's Ba' games: on Christmas Day 1945 and New Year's Day 1946. It's widely believed that the idea was scrapped because they were too violent!

Culture

Culture in Orkney

Orkney's rich and varied culture attracts thousands of visitors a year.
In addition to our fabulous award-winning galleries and museums, there's also a packed programme of local festivals with internationally acclaimed music, art, lectures and performances on offer throughout the year. Our new Orkney Theatre hosts drama productions and performances, and our network of community halls across the islands also play their part. We also have some uniquely Orcadian cultural spectacles, including the Christmas and New Year's Day Ba' games and the Festival of the Horse in August. Use the links below to find out more about some Orkney's main events and cultural celebrations.

Agricultural Shows

Orkney is famous for its agricultural shows which bring back absent Orcadians and attract visitors in great numbers.

The main event in the agricultural calendar is the County Show in Bignold Park in Kirkwall in August, attended by around 10,000 people – half of our population.

At this showcase, after more than a week of agricultural shows across Orkney - East Mainland, Dounby, Sanday, Shapinsay and the Hope Show - farmers come to parade their animals and hope for a show champion. As well as cattle there are top quality horses, sheep, goats and poultry competing for awards. There are also several horticultural societies which run their prize shows alongside the agricultural shows. After the shows, awards are handed out and celebrations get underway.

The shows are more than a day out for the farmers. They are a huge draw for families who enjoy seeing the animals, catching up with friends, and browsing at stalls selling locally produced crafts and goods, food produce, and country clothing or chatting at the fundraising tents and entering their competitions and raffles, or viewing the latest farm implements for sale. You'll normally find showjumping, dog trials, a fun fair, entertainment and food outlets at the shows too. All in all, a great day out!

The evening of County Show day sees the culmination of the fiercely contested Parish Cup football competition, with the final being played out in front of a passionate crowd by the two parishes who have reached this stage over a couple of months of qualifying rounds.

Later in the year the festivities continue at Harvest Homes across the county, celebratory ceilidhs which welcome all age groups.

Museums and Galleries

Orkney has a rich historical and artistic background, and the islands play host to a number of innovative, interesting and exciting museums and galleries. You can spend hours looking back at five thousand years of life in Orkney, and even see some of our artists and craft makers in action!

Orkney Art Galleries

Orkney's crystal clear air and magical northern light inspires many local artists and other creative souls who have been lured to our magical shores. There are enough art galleries here to keep visitors busy for weeks. Many have changing exhibitions and run courses. Other artists work in private studios but exhibit locally. A selection of galleries includes:

- ➢ Britt Harcus, artist and illustrator. Wellpark Garden Centre, Kirkwall

- Hoxa Tapestry Gallery, South Ronaldsay. Beautiful woven tapestries by Leila Thomson, other pieces by other family members
- Land Art, Papa Westray. Project exploring island landscape. Exhibitions and touring programmes
- Loft Gallery, St Margaret's Hope. Cooperative arts and crafts and exhibition space
- Northlight Studio and Gallery, Stromness. Work and short courses by tapestry artist Ros Bryant who also carves stone
- Peter Rowland Silversmith, Orphir. One-off commissions in gold and silver
- Shorelines Gallery, Finstown. Paintings and prints by Jane Glue
- Waterfront Gallery, Stromness. Crafts, paintings and prints by local artists. Exhibitions
- Wheeling Steen Gallery, Westray. Photographs and art by Edwin and Rosemary Rendall. Tearoom.
- Wildscape gallery, Stromness. Paintings of Orkney birds and landscapes by Tim Wootton

➤ Yellowbird Gallery, Birsay. Contemporary art. Landscapes by Lesley Murdoch, bird painting and bird and moth jewellery by Jon Thompson

Orkney Museums

Orkney's rich heritage and colourful history is told in its many museums through traditional display cases, interactive games and even farmhouses where you can dress up like our ancestors.

A must-see is Stromness Museum, the second oldest independent museum in Scotland, which showcases Orkney's strong maritime and natural history. Since 1837 the museum has curated treasures from around the world, many collected by Orkney seafarers and adventurers. The Victorian natural history gallery holds a stunning collection of bird eggs, fossils, sea creatures, mammals, butterflies and moths. You can find out about famous ships which sailed into Stromness including Captain Cook's Resolution and Endeavour and learn of Sir John Franklin's fateful journey. Arctic explorer Dr John Rae's links with Canadian native people and whale fishing have special exhibitions and you can see Robert Louis Stevenson's signature.

Orkney Museum in Tankerness House, Kirkwall, a fantastic laird's townhouse, is home to exhibits chronicling 5,500 years of Orkney's history from Neolithic times to modern social history. The photo archive is fascinating and you can see such treasures as a Viking grave plaque. There are temporary exhibitions too. Also in Kirkwall you can see a hangman's ladder and other interesting relics if you take a tour of the upper floors of St Magnus Cathedral. Orkney Wireless Museum in Kirkwall has an extensive collection of early domestic radio and wartime communication systems used in Orkney and also features early television sets. Knowledgeable staff are on hand to explain how equipment worked.

Two farm museums in West Mainland give a taste of the hard life on the land in Orkney. Corrigall Farm Museum in Harray is a traditional 'but and ben' house typical of the 19th century. There are hands-on activities for children, farmyard animals, peat fires, a working barn and grain kiln. You can take part in activities at certain times to learn ancient farming skills. Kirbuster Museum in Birsay is a 16th century homestead with a central hearth and stone neuk beds. Both have gardens to explore and gifts for sale.

As well as a huge fossil collection, the Fossil Museum and Heritage Centre in Burray features an exhibition about the building of the barriers and a local heritage museum. It also has a community tearoom with a great selection of homebakes.

Orkney's importance during two world wars is told at the Scapa Flow Visitor Centre and Museum at Lyness Pier on Hoy, right where the Houton ferry ties up. Inside wartime buildings and an oil storage tank you can watch film footage, view photographs listen to oral history accounts and see vehicles, weapons and historic boats.

The North Isles tell their stories too. Sanday has a heritage centre telling the story of the island, while Westray Heritage Centre is a mine of information with an archive to browse in, natural history displays and the Neolithic carved Westray Stone. Neighbouring Papa Westray's Bothy Museum at Holland Farm gives you a taste of old farming life with box beds and many interesting artefacts and is open free at all times. The Rousay Heritage Centre is another unmanned historical resource. There is even a Fairy Museum on Westray.

Pier Arts Centre

Voted the best building in Scotland in 2007, the Pier Arts Centre houses an important collection of British fine art donated to 'be held in trust for Orkney' by the author, peace activist and philanthropist Margaret Gardiner (1904–2005). The centre's permanent collection of 100 pieces includes work by Barbara Hepworth, Ben Nicolson and Alfred Wallis. There is also a year round programme of changing exhibitions, often national touring collections of contemporary art, and an annual open exhibition showcasing a huge range of art from the talented local artistic community. Artists in residence have been involved in innovative projects, often working with industry. The Pier Arts Centre also runs educational events for children and adults and hosts literature readings, gallery talks, small concerts and other events for local societies and groups. Gallery catalogues are published and are sold in the shop with other art books and upmarket merchandise and cards.

The centre first opened in 1978 and re-opened in July 2007 following a two year, £4.5 million Lottery funded redevelopment of its buildings. It is housed in buildings on one of the historic piers in Stromness right on the harbour's edge. Edward Clouston, a 19th century merchant and agent for the Hudson's Bay Company built an office and store on the pier. A drawing room from the house forms part of the centre which links historic buildings. In 2008 the Pier arts Centre was long listed for the Art Fund Prize for its sensitive and well received development.

Music in Orkney
Music appears to run in the blood in Orkney and is a way of life for many local people
You'll hear tunes played pretty much everywhere in Orkney - in homes, schools, pubs, churches, community halls and, during the

summer months, out in the streets. The Orkney Folk Festival is a huge draw for lovers of traditional music, with the St Magnus International Festival renowned worldwide for its classical programme, but smaller jazz and blues festivals are also growing in popularity.

Beyond the busy festival calendars you'll find ceilidh, pop and rock bands playing at weddings, charity gigs, harvest homes, Christmas dos and work get-togethers. It's true to say that most celebrations in Orkney involve a dance, with live music always the preferred option.

There are always visiting artists and bands heading to the islands. In the recent past there have been performances by the likes of Mumford and Sons, Idlewild, Steve Earle and Ricky Ross.

Several local projects and initiatives are working hard to save Orkney's rich musical traditions from extinction, ensuring future generations can enjoy the distinctive Orcadian tunes of the past. Orkney Traditional Music Project and the Orkney Strathspey and Reel Society involve large groups of people playing and sometimes performing, with new members always welcome to sit in on sessions. The Big Orkney Song Project has collected and recorded more than 1000 Orkney songs, which can be heard at the Orkney Library and Archive in Kirkwall.

There is a long tradition of fiddle music in the islands and the majority of Orkney schoolchildren get the opportunity to play the violin, or another instrument, from an early age.

Orkney is home to several choirs, pipe bands and orchestras, as well as accomplished solo singers and a huge number of bands, playing everything from traditional and modern folk, to country, jazz, heavy rock, swing, ballads and the blues.

Orkney Folk Festival

Orkney Folk Festival is a firmly established date in Scotland's folk festival calendar and has drawn visitors back to the isands many times since it started in 1982.

Involving a heady mix of international and UK artists and performances from fine local talent, the Orkney Folk Festival plays an important part in the musical and cultural life of Orkney.

Words just can't do it justice though – experience of 2014 Festival...

Held over four days at the end of May, the festival offers folk music in its broadest sense to please all tastes, from acoustic singing and traditional tunes, to concerts featuring contemporary bands and dance gigs. Ceilidhs in parish halls and community centres offer a taste of traditional island life with a concert, supper and dance. Centred on

Stromness, where opening and farewell concerts are held, venues include the town hall, Stromness Academy, Stromness Hotel and the Pier Arts Centre.

The town's pubs host jam sessions which often spill out onto the street if the weather is fine. And walking down the town's long street, you'll often hear music emanating from windows and gardens. An annual open stage event has spawned several successful music careers, with workshops in playing and song writing also hugely popular. Not just confined to Stromness, folk festival artists travel to perform in the isles, parishes and even in Kirkwall too. Another regular event at the festival is the visitors versus locals comedy football match, which is short on actual folk music, but high on laughs

Orkney Science Festival

Orkney International Science Festival has been a part of the calendar every September since 1991 and has something for everyone.

You don't have to be into science to enjoy this festival which has Entertainment with a big E written large. There is a package of family-friendly activities, food and drink events and music as well as thought-provoking lectures on offer. Astronomy and time travel, archaeology and polar exploration, the science of everyday things and even a courtroom drama starring real pathologists have all been acted out. There have been experiments to keep the boffins happy and banquets, whisky tasting and ceilidhs to keep body and soul together. Science themes in art and literature have also been explored at past festivals.

The festival is truly international with guest speakers from around the world. Groundbreaking and fresh ideas have been debated and revealed at events, spellbinding audiences. Events are held throughout Orkney including the smaller islands. And schools get involved too with more than a thousand pupils benefitting.

The seven day festival is traditionally held at the beginning of September and puts Orkney firmly on the map after the school holidays. It's well worth a visit after the summer rush is over. Prepare to be highly entertained.

St Magnus International Festival

The St Magnus International Festival is one of the UK's leading arts festivals and is held over six days during the Orkney midsummer.

The festival was founded in 1977 by Orkney-based composer, and Master of the Queen's Music, Sir Peter Maxwell Davies. The inaugural festival featured his opera The Martyrdom of St Magnus, based on the novel Magnus, by the late Orcadian writer George Mackay Brown. The festival continues to commission new work from established and young composers.

International orchestras and soloists, theatre and dance companies, poets and authors, bands and visual artists all perform at the event, alongside community participants. Visiting artists hold materclasses in schools, while conducting and composing courses are open to audiences. The locally formed Festival Chorus performs major work, with its input into concerts always a highlight. The late Alan Plater wrote plays for and attended two festivals, while many top musicians have travelled to Orkney to take part, including André Previn, Julian Bream and Evelyn Glennie.

The festival's venues range from the large space of St Magnus Cathedral to the tiny Italian Chapel, and from the Pickaquoy Centre's huge concert arena to small parish halls. Productions premiered in Orkney at St Magnus International Festival have gone on to tour at other major events, including the Edinburgh Fringe. And Orkney has its own festival fringe, the Magfest, which offers a range of exciting events, from drama and circus, to cabaret and music. Always a brilliant end to the day, the Festival Club offers the chance for artists, visitors and locals to relax and reflect together.

Other Festivals in Orkney

From jazz and blues, to wine and storytelling, Orkney has a packed programme of smaller festivals to suit everyone.

One of the first mini festivals of the year is Papay Gyro Nights Art Festival, a fairly recent revival of an old Papay tradition, which is held at the time of the first full moon in February. Next it's the Orkney Jazz Festival, staged during the last weekend of April at the Stromness Hotel and featuring mainly traditional jazz from visiting performers.

May brings the Orkney Nature Festival, which was launched in 2013. It offers the chance to take advantage of Orkney's wildlife, with boat cruises, walks, talks - and even the chance to go kayaking and rockpooling with experts.

The first week of June sees Orkney play host to Scotland's only wine festival, held at various restaurants around the county. Tastings, lunches, dinners and talks are tutored by visiting winemakers and merchants, making the Orkney Wine Festival a real highlight of the year for both wine lovers and foodies.

Stromness Shopping Week has been held during the third week of July for more than 60 years. This community wide spectacle, originally introduced to entice people into local shops, now involves a host of family and sporting events, along with a huge range of activities and shows from visiting performers and bands. It all ends with an eagerly anticipated fancy dress parade, a fireworks display over the town's harbour and a dance in the street.

Further afield you can have a truly entertaining time at the Papa Westray Fun Weekend with an adult and children's sports day, carty racing down the brae and two ceilidhs. The Westray Sailing Regatta is another firm favourite for visitors to the isles.

August is a time of festival fever in Orkney. In addition to the agricultural shows, you can watch Kirkwall Sailing Regatta, tour the Vintage Rally Show and watch the Riding of the Marches in Kirkwall. For a spectacle you will see nowhere else don't miss the South Ronaldsay Boys' Ploughing Match & Festival of the Horse. Children dress in intricate horse costumes at St Margaret's Hope and boys compete with mini ploughs on the Sands o'Wright beach.

In September the Orkney Blues Festival showcases blues in its broadest interpretation with visiting bands and local talent performing in several venues around Stromness for a non-stop blues experience.

The Orcadian Story Trust runs the Orkney Storytelling Festival at the end of October, which features international storytellers as well as local experts in this ancient art form. Many featured stories have been passed down through generations and cover Orkney's past right back to its very creation, as told in the story of Assipattle.

Travel and Tourism

Orkney is a land of rolling green fields, rugged coastlines and spectacular pristine beaches

Approximately seventy islands and skerries make up Orkney, with up to 20 of those inhabited. Most of the 21,000 strong population live on the largest island, the mainland, though many of the inner and outer islands of Orkney also support thriving communities, each with its own distinct identity.

The Orkney capital Kirkwall - officially a city and Royal Burgh - is home to around 9,000 people, while some 2,000 live in the picturesque harbour town of Stromness, in Orkney's west mainland.

The lush and fertile Orkney landscape supports a thriving agricultural industry, with production of high quality beef cattle the local speciality. Sheep and dairy farming are also key activities, with the bulk of locally produced milk being used by the islands' acclaimed cheese and ice-cream makers. The clean seas around Orkney sustain a small but vital fisheries and aquaculture industry, with crab, lobster, scallops and salmon a particular focus.

Orkney's many food and drink producers take their role as ambassadors very seriously, with quality and taste the bywords in an industry that has firmly established the islands as paradise for food lovers. In addition to the famed beef, lamb, salmon and shellfish, there's the prized meat that comes from the legendary seaweed fed sheep of North Ronaldsay, along with cheese, oatcakes, fudge, beer, whisky, ice cream, wine and a multitude of other locally produced treats.

Given Orkney's incredible scenery, abundant wildlife and mind-boggling wealth of archaeological sites, it's no surprise to learn that tourism is also a hugely important industry in the islands. Tens of thousands of visitors enjoy holidays and tours in the islands each year and Orkney remains the top UK destination for cruise liners.

The people of Orkney have always been practical, but with a real eye for the aesthetic. That could explain why the islands have the highest concentration of craft jewellers in the UK. Whilst many of the manufacturers draw inspiration for their work from Orkney's landscape and history, each is unique and the variety of jewellery on offer locally is dazzling. Orkney's arts and crafts scene as a whole is a thriving one, with a huge number of businesses covering everything from pottery and woodwork, to textiles, knitwear, artwork and photography.

Recent years have seen Orkney become an important international centre in the emerging renewable energy industry. Wind power, as one might imagine, is a long established technology in the islands, but now Orkney is also at the forefront of pioneering developments in wave and tidal energy. The European Marine Energy Centre, based near Stromness, is the world's first and only full-scale test laboratory for wave and tidal devices, attracting developers from around the globe. This new industry is already having a positive impact in the islands, supporting hundreds of jobs in the marine energy supply chain sector.

Getting to Orkney

Getting to Orkney is straightforward, with modern, fast and reliable transport links connecting the islands with the rest of the world.
Orkney is closer than you might think and extremely well connected.
Travelling to Orkney:

By air – Flybe flights are operated by Loganair from Glasgow (80 minutes), Edinburgh (80 minutes), Inverness (45 minutes), Aberdeen (50 minutes) and Shetland (35 minutes); most have good links to other national airports.

By car - If you wish to drive, head north to the ferry ports of either Aberdeen, Scrabster, Gills Bay, or John O'Groats (passenger ferry only May-September).

By sea – There are three main vehicle ferry routes to and from Orkney. NorthLink Ferries sail between Lerwick in Shetland, Hatston in Kirkwall and Aberdeen, with the company also operating the 90 minute service between Scrabster and Stromness. A quicker option again is the Pentland Ferries catamaran, which sails between Gill's Bay, near John o' Groats, and St Margaret's Hope in South Ronaldsay (just over 1 hour).

By bus - Citylink buses run to Aberdeen, Thurso and Gills Bay, with ongoing ferry connections to Orkney. The Orkney Bus, which travels direct from Inverness to Kirkwall and utilises the John O' Groats passenger ferry link, runs between June and the start of September.

By train - Travel by train to Aberdeen or Thurso, where you can catch a ferry to Orkney from the harbours listed above. More information on train timetables can be found on the ScotRail or National Rail websites.

Orkney residents are eligible for discounted fares on Flybe and Northlink through the Air Discount Scheme and the Islander discounts.

Relocating your business to Orkney:
Moving your business to Orkney couldn't be simpler, with many local shipping and haulage firms offering fast and efficient relocation and storage services. They'll transport and deliver goods from mainland Britain to the islands and can organise shipment from other countries. Transport throughout Orkney, including between islands, can also be easily arranged.

Life in Orkney

Life in Orkney very Exciting.
With our friendly, busy communities, superb sports and leisure facilities, top class education and health care systems, and a thriving arts and culture scene, Orkney offers a quality of life that's hard to match.

Getting around on Orkney's quiet roads is enjoyable rather than frustrating, as it can be on the clogged-up roads of the UK mainland, with excellent bus and inter-island ferry services ensuring all corners of the islands are accessible. And a wide range of housing is available to buy, from traditional stone homes to modern eco dwellings. Private landlords offer a variety of properties to rent, with social housing provided by Orkney Housing Association and Orkney Islands Council.

Our schools regularly top national league tables and many of our young people go on to study at college or university - Orkney College is part of the University of the Highlands and Islands campus and Heriot Watt University also has a campus in Stromness. Others decide to pursue opportunities in Orkney's diverse business community, whether in agriculture, fisheries, construction, finance, hospitality, tourism, catering, the arts or crafts.

Local health needs are catered for by NHS Orkney, which has links to hospitals and specialists throughout the country, with a brand new hospital set to open in Orkney in 2018.

Orkney has countless clubs and societies who are always on the lookout for new members. Our sports and leisure facilities are also second to none, with everything from swimming to golf on offer, even in the outlying islands. Whatever your sport or hobby, chances are you'll find others in Orkney who share your passion.

A Prepared Welcome

Orkney has a lot going for it - beautiful scenery, friendly people, a strong community spirit. It's also a vibrant and thriving place with a wide range of industries and jobs.

If you want to make Orkney your new home you'll find plenty of help and advice on offer locally. In this section, we've brought together information about day to day life in Orkney that you might find useful - from health and education services, to local clubs and sports and leisure facilities. Use the links below or on the side panel to find out more about what life in Orkney is like, and why it might be for you

Clubs in Orkney

Orkney has an extremely lively club and society scene, covering everything from bridge to pipe bands and kick boxing to karate. There really is something for every interest

There are a huge number of clubs to join in Orkney and there are usually no long waiting lists or hefty fees to fork out. Clubs are keen to welcome new members and there is always scope to start a new one in the unlikely event that your hobby or interest is not already catered for.

Clubs in Orkney include many of the following in parishes, towns and islands: camera; cycling; gardening; flowers; crafts; chess; bridge;

riding; pony clubs; carriage driving; flying; pool; snooker; motorsports; sailing (including dinghy, Orkney yoles); sea angling; loch fishing; modelling; many drama groups; pipe bands; music associations; writing groups; reading groups; golf clubs; triathlon; athletics; kick boxing; karate; kayaking; football; rugby; cricket; badminton; squash; swimming; darts league; fitness; wind surfing; rowing; archery; hockey; bowling; climbing; vintage motoring; cadets; Brownies and Guides; Scouts; Boys' Brigade, Royal British Legions; ramblers; 18 youth clubs; 14 senior citizen clubs; U3A; the Orkney Federation of SWRIs; wildlife and parish hall and community associations. Hopefully, something for everyone!

Many of the clubs' details are on the Orkney Communities website and guide or are listed in local libraries with contact details for membership secretaries. The events and activities of many of the clubs are advertised in newsletters, websites, posters and the press. BBC Radio Orkney broadasts a daily diary of community events, and publishes it on the station's Facebook page.

Events include exhibitions, sailing regattas, fishing competitions, sports matches, including the annual Orkney Rugby Club Sevens tournament in May, the Hoy Half Marathon in June and regular stage performances. There are golf clubs in Kirkwall, Stromness, South

Ronaldsay, Sanday, Westray and Papa Westray. Orkney football and rugby teams play in Scottish leagues so many weekends through the winter there are exciting matches to watch or to travel away to.

Health and Social Care.

Orkney has excellent health and social care services, with a number of modern facilities - and even a brand new hospital earmarked to open in 2018.

A wide range of health services in Orkney are delivered by NHS Orkney with some specialist services provided on mainland Scotland by other health boards such as NHS Grampian in Aberdeen and NHS Highland in Inverness. NHS Orkney is the smallest health board in Scotland but is responsible for providing many of the services that the larger health boards do.

Balfour Hospital in Kirkwall has six wards, a day hospital, a day surgery unit and departments including physiotherapy, occupational therapy, casualty, outpatients, audiology, radiography, pharmacy, an oral surgery unit, a decontamination unit and a new CT scanner. There are three consultant surgeons delivering general surgery. Patients do not always need to travel south for consultations as telemedicine means video conferencing can be used when appropriate. Specialists also travel to Orkney to conduct clinics and cut down on waiting times and referrals for patients having to travel. Plans for a new hospital in Kirkwall are well underway, with a completion date set for 2018.

Patients who do travel south have their transport arranged through their GP and can choose to go by plane or boat. Patients who need emergency treatment that cannot be delivered in Orkney are transported by Scottish Air Ambulance which operates fixed wing aircraft based in Aberdeen and Glasgow and helicopters based in Glasgow and Inverness. Back-up is supplied when needed by the MoD and coastguard.

GP services with nurse practitioners attached are delivered in two surgeries in Kirkwall and surgeries and clinics in Stromness, Dounby, St Margaret's Hope, Evie, Eday, Rousay, Stronsay, North Ronaldsay, Sanday, Shapinsay, Longhope and Westray. Papa Westray, Flotta and Eday have no resident GP but do have visiting doctors and nurses. School nurses and health visitors work through the Children's Services Department.

Orkney also has a number of NHS and private dental practices, which accept new registrations.

Orkney Islands Council provides a range of community social services and runs a number of modern and fully equipped care centres across the islands. Through Orkney Health and Care, a joint body with NHS Orkney, it also provides mental health services, drug and alcohol advice, learning disability services, services for older people and sexual health services.

Complementary health therapists offer a wide range of services in Orkney too.

Education

Orkney has around three thousand pupils across its seventeen primary schools, three junior highs and two secondary schools. There's a halls of residence for pupils from the islands to attend school in Kirkwall and further and higher education is available at Orkney College UHI and at the Heriot Watt University campus in Stromness.

Orkney schools are run by Orkney Islands Council's Education, Leisure and Housing Department and a child's whole school life, from pre-school right through to further and higher education, may be undertaken in the county. Orkney's secondary schools frequently feature in the top 100 Best State School lists and individual schools have also achieved top marks through HM Inspectorate of Education reports.

For the early days there are two nurseries in Kirkwall offering education for children from the age of two, and most of the county's primary schools offer nursery and pre-school provision. Childcare and baby and toddler groups are also available. There are two senior secondary schools: Kirkwall Grammar School and Stromness Academy; and three junior high schools: Westray, Stronsay and Sanday, which cater from nursery up to 4th year of secondary. After that the North Isles pupils stay in halls of residence in Kirkwall and attend Kirkwall Grammar School, both of which can boast brand new state-of-the-art premises opened at the beginning of 2014, and fantastic new facilities for the area.

To enrol your child in any of Orkney's schools, contact the head teacher in your catchment area, listed on the Orkney Islands Council website. You can also request a place at an alternative school. School transport is available for pupils living a distance away from school within their catchment area.

Orkney College offers further and higher education and degree and post graduate learning. It is a constituent college of the University of the Highlands and Islands (UHI). Courses include Scottish Vocational Qualifications, Scottish Group Awards, the Higher National Certificate and Diploma, degrees and post graduate courses and Ph.D supervision. There are also evening classes and short courses. Subjects include agriculture, archaeology, art and design, business studies, care, carpentry and joinery, cultural studies, hospitality, IT, marine and Nordic studies. Learning centres are scattered throughout Orkney with the core centre at Orkney College. Learning can be accessed through video conferencing and online by people living in remote areas.

Heriot Watt University's Orkney campus, the International Centre for Island Technology, is located in Stromness, and provides post graduate level education in a range of renewable energy subjects.

Sport and Leisure

Orkney has some of the best sports and leisure facilities anywhere in the country - perfect to relax and unwind after a day's work. You can also take advantage of fitness classes, gyms and swimming pools - as well as the great outdoors - if you want to get active.

The main venue for leisure in the county is the Pickaquoy Centre in Kirkwall, which offers sports, arts and leisure activities. Known locally as 'the Picky', the centre also hosts major concerts, gigs, performances and sporting competitions. The New Phoenix Cinema shows blockbusters (in 2D and 3D), world films. live theatre performances via satellite link and seats 243 people.

Picky's Exercise Zone offers many classes including Body Pump, Body Combat and Body Balance, yoga, cardio cycle, Metafit and Zumba. The Fitness Zone is a fully equipped gym with all the equipment you'd expect: treadmills, bikes and steppers etc. You need a short induction to be able to use the gym. For a more relaxing time the Health Zone has a spa pool, sauna, steam room and plunge shower. Beauty therapists offer a range of treatments such as facials, body wraps and manicures whilst health therapists treat using methods such as Reiki, reflexology and podiatry. Children aged ten and under can let off steam in Jungle World indoor play area or have a laser combat game or use the play park outside. Also outside are all-weather and grass sports pitches, used for rugby and football, an artificial cricket wicket and an athletics track. An extension to Picky saw a brand new six lane swimming pool, leisure pool and squash courts open in 2013.

There are plenty of other swimming pools in Orkney too. The Stromness pool was Orkney's first, opening in 1969, and now includes a steam room, sauna, spa and fitness centre. There are also smaller pools in the islands of Hoy, Westray, Sanday and Stronsay.

The new Kirkwall Grammar School also offers a range of fitness classes and a fitness suite and here you can also hire the games hall, gym and dance studio for club activities. There are also floodlit 3G sports pitches at Kirkwall Grammar School and at Stromness Academy.

A number of people offer fitness classes throughout the mainland and the islands and there are seven Healthy Living Centres in Orkney which provide small gyms. Members must be trained to use the equipment and a buddy system operates. They are located at St Margaret's Hope in South Ronaldsay, in North Walls in Hoy, and in Rousay, Sanday, Shapinsay, Stronsay and Westray.

There are play parks throughout the isles and sports areas at the Market Green in Stromness and the Bignold Park in Kirkwall. There are many sporting activities in Orkney and competitive sports are played against teams and sportsmen and women from outwith Orkney and even internationally, as in the Island Games. Many sports activities and clubs are listed on the Orkney Communities website clubs page. Sports include football, rugby, cricket, golf, triathlon, cycling, martial arts, bowling, bowls, athletics and hockey. Tankerness House Gardens is an attractive and sheltered location for a relaxing stop behind the Orkney Museum. There are also a small number of allotments for hire in Kirkwall and Stromness, through Orkney Islands Council.

Community centres and halls in Orkney also offer many sporting and leisure facilities with club nights such as badminton and five-a-side football, as well as functions and drama groups. Halls may also be hired by individuals and groups.

Other leisure services include Orkney Library and Archive. The main library and archive is in Kirkwall and the other library is in Stromness. Both have reading groups and Stromness has a writing group too. There are story times for children, newspapers and magazines, CDs and DVDs to hire, free wifi access, computers, an online catalogue and even an online reading group. You can study local history through primary sources in the archive, trace your family tree with the Orkney Family History Society, view images in the photographic archive and listening to recordings in the sound archive. The library service also operates mobile vans which take books to all the north and south isles which have ro-ro ferries. Boxes of books are delivered to housebound library members. Orkney also has several museums with permanent displays and special exhibitions and events.

Leisure activities are run by the council and many clubs, groups and organisations across Orkney. For example, the RSPB in Orkney runs events and guided walks on its reserves to catch a glimpse of birds and other wildlife. Historic Scotland's Ranger Service hosts guided walks around sites such as the Ring of Brodgar. Island rangers take groups on specialist wildlife or history walks. The possibilities for leisure activities in Orkney are many and extend to sailing, rock climbing, diving and cycling or just walking in one of the most beautiful landscapes in Britain.

Events in Orkney

Orkney has a packed calendar of events running for much of the year, with our many festivals among the top attraction for visitors and residents alike.

Kicking things off in March is the Orkney One Act Play Festival, which sees Orkney's local drama groups competing for a place in the Scottish Community Drama Association's (SCDA) divisional and national contests.

Stromness hosts the Orkney Jazz Festival in April, with celebrations for Orkney's patron saint, St Magnus, taking place on the 16th of the month. Orkney's famous folk festival is held towards the end of May, with some of the best traditional musicians in the world sharing a platform with our local talent. On Norwegian Constitution Day - May 17 - there's a parade, service and dance in Kirkwall to celebrate Orkney's Norse heritage with our visiting friends from across the North Sea.

The internationally acclaimed St Magnus International Festival takes place in June, with performances from leading classical musicians, singers, orchestras and poets. Scotland's only wine festival is also staged here in June, as are traditional midnight golf matches that make the most of Orkney's light summer nights. Stromness Shopping Week in July offers a whole week of entertainment for all the family, with a spectacular pier-head fireworks display and dance concluding this ever popular event.

There's no let up in August when the agricultural shows, held throughout the county, allow Orkney's farmers to show off their champion animals. The shows are hugely popular days out for all the family, drawing exiled Orcadians back to the islands, along with many visitors. The Vintage Rally Show and the Riding of the Marches in Kirkwall are held after the County Show has taken place. Another event is the unique Festival of the Horse and Boys' Ploughing Match in South Ronaldsay.

The Orkney International Science Festival, held in September, has grown in popularity with many of the fascinating talks and events sold out each year. Later in the month Stromness hosts the Orkney Blues Festival, with the town's bars the focus for gigs from local and visiting groups.

If you like to hear a good traditional tale, delivered by some of the best storytellers in the business, then October's Orkney Storytelling Festival has much to offer.

And for three weeks either side of the winter solstice on December 21 you can witness the light from the setting sun in the Neolithic tomb of Maeshowe. Christmas concerts and the lighting of the Christmas lights in all the parishes and isles are an opportunity for communities to get together in the dark days of winter.

On Christmas Day and New Year's Day the famous Ba' is played in Kirkwall in a men's and a boys' version. It s a serious business, reserved for those who know what they're doing, with games usually lasting for several hours.

Between the festivals there are many concerts, talks, art exhibitions, plays, operas, gigs, shows, sporting events and all manner of other activities taking place. In fact, you'd be hard pressed to find a week in the Orkney calendar when nothing was happening, so there's never a dull moment!

Housing in Orkney

Orkney has a good selection of houses to buy or rent, with part rent/ownership schemes also available. Property prices in the islands are generally lower than the Scottish average, while the quality of life here remains high.

Houses for sale are marketed by local solicitors who advertise them through their offices in Kirkwall and Stromness, online, through property websites and in the local press. There are houses to suit all tastes and budgets, from grand town residences and on street apartments to large country properties with land and outbuildings.

Small and sturdy stone built dwellings were built by Orcadians of the past to withstand whatever the weather threw at them, but modern bungalows and Scandinavian-style wooden chalets will keep out the elements too. Out in the isles you may find a ruined building to buy as a Grand Designs style project and there are plots of land for sale with planning consent for building. Limited grants or support may be available for the renovation of older buildings and for projects that use renewable and sustainable energy. There are also often businesses such as hotels and retail units for sale with living accommodation.

Private landlords rent out furnished and unfurnished properties as long lets, particularly during the quieter winter months and this can be a useful stop gap for people relocating to Orkney.

Orkney Housing Association Ltd (OHAL) was established in 1985 to complement the local council's housing stock. In recent years hundreds of homes have been built in Orkney through the local authority building programme, and a series of private developments and sites have also been available.

Property for Sale

Whether you are looking to buy a house, a flat, a cottage, a traditional or a modern home, a farm, a shop or another business - in an island or mainland location, you will find it here. All Orkney properties listed for sale or for rent with local agents are searchable here in one handy location.

Marcella, 31 Rope Walk, Kirkwall, KW15 1XJ

Kirkwall

Offers Over £155,000

3 Bedrooms

Marcella is a well-presented 3 bedroom semi-detached bungalow situated in a popular residential area on the outskirts of Kirkwall. The attractive property has garden to the front, side and rear together with a spacious detached garage.

Erisian, 4 Meadow Crescent, Kirkwall, KW15 1HA

Kirkwall

Offers Over £180,000

3 Bedrooms

This well-presented modern 3 bedroom dwellinghouse offers a high standard of family accommodation and is conveniently situated close to the schools. The attractive property stands in good decorative order and has air source heating together with air to water central heating with under floor on the ground floor and radiators on the first floor. The interior features light oak doors and there are UPVC framed double glazed windows together with matching exterior doors.

Rango Cottage, Sandwick, KW16 3JB

West Mainland

FOR SALE £150,000

3 Bedrooms

This well presented three bedroom dwellinghouse is situated in the parish of Sandwick. The property has an outbuilding, various sheds and a lovely sheltered garden to the rear. Nice views over the surrounding farmland and over Harray Loch to the front. Accommodation comprises Living room, Dining Kitchen, Bathroom, three Bedrooms and a Shower room.

Oakhurst, Willow Road, Kirkwall, KW15 1NJ

Kirkwall

CLOSING DATE £135,000

2 Bedrooms

CLOSING DATE 12NOON TUESDAY 3rd OCTOBER* This lovely two bedroom semi-detached house with a beautiful mature walled garden is located in a desirable area a short walk to the town centre and all local amenities. Accommodation comprises Living room, Kitchen, Utility room, WC, Bathroom and two Bedrooms.

Crompton, St Mary's, Holm, KW17 2RT

East Mainland, South Ronaldsay and Burray

Offers Over £165,000

3 Bedrooms

Crompton is a 3 bedroom detached bungalow situated in the picturesque village of St Mary's. The dwellinghouse has oil fired central heating and UPVC framed double glazed windows.

Upper Flat, 22 Garden Street, Kirkwall, KW15 1JA

Kirkwall

Offers Around £95,000

2 Bedrooms

This spacious first and attic floor flat is situated very close to the town centre. The property has a shared vestibule with a private door leading to the stairs up to the landing.

6 Old Scapa Road, Kirkwall, KW15 1BB

Kirkwall

Offers Over £335,000

4 Bedrooms

6 Old Scapa Road is a distinctive 4 bedroom detached dwellinghouse offering spacious accommodation on three floors. The attractive property has been tastefully modernised and extended, and also features a mature sheltered rear garden. The original property dates from approximately 1800 and the extension was added in 2008. The property is 'C' listed.

Mucklehame, Swannay, KW17 2NS

West Mainland

REVISED PRICE £295,000

5 Bedrooms

OPEN VIEWING 2 - 4pm SATURDAY 14th OCTOBER Mucklehame is a spacious five bedroom detached dwellinghouse with integral double garage, presented to a very high standard and enjoying a countryside location with beautiful open views. Accommodation comprises Entrance Vestibule, Hallway, Living room, Dining Kitchen, Utility Room, Bathroom and four Bedrooms, one with an En-suite and Dressing room on the Ground Floor. Den/Fifth Bedroom situated on the First Floor.

South Ness, 8 acres or thereby, North Ronaldsay, KW17 2BE

North Isles

Offers Over £35,000

South Ness is a registered croft and includes a former dwellinghouse and range of traditional outbuildings which require renovation and modernisation together with a static caravan and 8 acres or thereby.

10 Jib Park, Finstown, KW17 2HJ

West Mainland

Offers Over £195,000

3 Bedrooms

10 Jib Park is a well-presented 3 bedroom detached bungalow situated in a cul-de-sac on the outskirts of the picturescue village of Finstown. The bungalow has a spacious integral garage and a large garden which extends to one side.

Vinya Heim, Former School and Schoolhouse, Deerness, KW17 2QQ

East Mainland, South Ronaldsay and Burray

REVISED PRICE £195,000

3 Bedrooms

Offered for sale is this former schoolhouse and school with a garage and several outbuildings situated in the lovely parish of Deerness. The schoolhouse has been lovingly renovated to create a desirable three bedroom family home. The attached school requires renovation and is entirely adaptable and could be utilised as a workshop, craft/art studio or equally altered for additional or separate accommodation with the appropriate planning consents. Owing to ill health the sellers have reduced the price.

Hestigar, 7 St Rognvald's Way, Kirkwall, KW15 1SQ

Kirkwall

Offers Over £165,000

3 Bedrooms

Hestigar is a three bedroom detached bungalow situated in a private cul-de-sac.

Failte, Bignold Park Road, Kirkwall, KW15 1PT

Kirkwall

Offers Over £175,000

3 Bedrooms

Failte is a spacious 3 bedroom detached dwellinghouse conveniently situated within walking distance of the town centre and schools. The well-presented bungalow has oil central heating and UPVC and wooden framed double glazed windows.

Meerblick, Holm, KW17 2SB

East Mainland, South Ronaldsay and Burray

Offers Over £365,000

5 Bedrooms

Meerblick is a spacious modern 4 bedroom bungalow designed to capture the natural light and the beautiful sea views. The U shaped property offers a high standard of accommodation and is very energy efficient.

13 King Street, Kirkwall, KW15 1JF

Kirkwall

UNDER OFFER £120,000

2 Bedrooms

Beautifully presented two bedroom mid-terraced house situated in the heart of Kirkwall with all amenities close by. Accommodation comprises Living room, Kitchen and Shower room on the lower floor and two double Bedrooms on the upper. Perfect for a first time buyer or property investor.

Rothiesholm, 26 Bignold Park Road, Kirkwall, KW15 1PT

Kirkwall

FOR SALE £210,000

3 Bedrooms

This lovely two/three bedroom detached house with a garage, car port, store and large garden is located in a desirable area, close to the schools and a short walk to the town centre. Accommodation comprises Living room, Kitchen, Pantry, Bathroom, two/three Bedrooms and a Shower room.

Stockan, Sandwick, KW16 3JB

West Mainland

FOR SALE £155,000

2 Bedrooms

Stockan is a well presented two bedroom bungalow enjoying lovely views over the surrounding farmland with the Hoy Hills in the distance. The property has a spacious hallway which would allow for a staircase to be introduced to the attic space which has been floored and configured in preparation of future conversion of further accommodation. Accommodation comprises Vestibule, Main Hallway, Living Room, Kitchen, Sun Porch, two Bedrooms and a Shower room.

Sunnyside, extending to 1.12 acres or thereby, Petertown Road, Orphir, KW17 2RE

West Mainland

Offers Over £160,000

3 Bedrooms

This 3 bedroom bungalow was tastefully modernised and extended several years ago and enjoys a beautiful panoramic view across farmland and sea with the Hoy Hills, Graemsay and Stromness in the distance.

B listed 3 bedroom end terrace dwelling situated only a short walk to the town centre with all ...

Kirkwall

Offers Over £65,000

3 Bedrooms

B listed 3 bedroom end terrace dwelling situated only a short walk to the town centre with all local amenities.

The property has a combination of hardwood double glazed and UPVC double glazed windows and electric storage heating with an open fire in the sitting room.

21 St Catherine's Place requires extensive rencvations throughout but offers great potential for the buy to let market.

Outside there is a shared garden to the rear w th a shared drying area and a garden shed.

Accommodation comprises of entrance porch, hall, sitting room and kitchen/diner on the ground floor with three bedrooms and a bathroom on the first floor.

Conyar, 5 acres or thereby, Harray, KW17 2LF

West Mainland

Offers Over £325,000

4 Bedrooms

Conyar is a beautiful 4 bedroom detached bungalow offering an outstanding view over farmland with the Loch of Harray and Hoy Hills in the distance. The spacious property was tastefully renovated and extended (completed c2013), to a very high standard, and viewing is essential to fully appreciate its fine qualities and location.

Achnagowan, Innertown, Stromness, KW16 3JP

Stromness

UNDER OFFER £360,000

5 Bedrooms

Achnagowan is a five bedroom dwellinghouse with an integral double garage offering a high standard of spacious accommodation and breathtaking panoramic views over Scapa Flow, the Hoy Hills and the Pentland Firth. Accommodation comprises Living room, Kitchen,

Dining room, Sun Lounge, Utility room, five Bedrooms with one en-suite, two Bathrooms, Wet room, two Studies and a Playroom.

Glenfyne, Holm Road, Kirkwall, KW15 1RX

Kirkwall & St Ola

UNDER OFFER £160,000

4 Bedrooms

This well presented four bedroom semi-detached dwellinghouse is situated on the outskirts of Kirkwall with lovely views to the rear over Kirkwall and within walking distance of the schools, hospital and town centre. Accommodation comprises Living room, Dining Kitchen, Utility room, four Bedrooms and a Bathroom

Shopping in Orkney

Orkney is heaven for shoppers. You can pick up some of the very best local food and drink products, high quality jewellery, original arts and crafts and goods from chain supermarkets - all on one short trip.

Unlike many rural towns, Kirkwall and Stromness can boast main streets full of independent retailers, from long established grocers, bakers and jewellers to more recent wine, music and book shops and designer shops selling their own textiles, accessories, jewellery, art and other crafts. Orkney also has fantastic country and island shops, stocking everything you need to save you a trip into the two main towns.

Many of our craft and gift shops stock brands from outwith the area, as well as their own designs and those of other local producers. You'll be amazed at the vast and sometimes unexpected ranges stocked by some of our traditional shops. There are butchers, bakers, fishmongers and delicatessens, stocking the very best in local produce.

We have lots for you to see as you wander through our towns and plenty of wonderful cafes and restaurants to take a break in.

Out and about, you can visit our craft workshops on the craft trail and buy beautifully crafted pieces right where they were made.

There is so much choice that there is often no need to visit the major retailers, but we also have these by way of a major Tesco store, Lidl, M&Co and Boots in Kirkwall and a number of Co-op shops in Kirkwall, Stromness and Dounby.

Transport in Orkney

Orkney's buses and ferries are vital lifelines for those who live, work and travel to school in our parishes, towns and isles.

Orkney Islands Council coordinates public transport services within Orkney and is also responsible for maintaining car parks and roads. It is also working to promote alternative forms of transport such as car sharing, walking and cycling.

Buses

Stagecoach operates most of the public bus routes on mainland Orkney. Routes cover St Margaret's Hope, Holm, Kirkwall, Finstown to Stromness, Kirkwall to Birsay, Houton, Deerness, Kirkwall Airport, Hatston Pier, Tingwall Pier, Dounby and Harray. Kirkwall Travel Centre is the main bus hub with a waiting area, luggage lockers and an information desk. There is also a travel centre in Stromness at the ferry terminal. Timetables are displayed at the travel centres, bus stops and on the council website. More information is available by telephoning Stagecoach in Orkney on 01856 878014. Buses link with ferries to and from other islands and inter-isles flights, as well as ferries and flights to mainland Scotland. You can hail and ride a bus in Orkney outside town by waiting at a safe point.

There are also demand responsive services run by the Orkney Community Transport Organisation (OCTO) on 01856 871515. Dial-a-Bus operated by Orkney Disability Forum runs a door to door service for people who are disabled, have mobility problems or are aged over

60. Bookings must be made 24 hours in advance by telephoning 01856 871515.

Isles buses operate on some of the outlying isles. The Eday Bus runs on a Thursday and is an on demand service linking with the ferry. Contact 01857 622206 for booking. The Rousay Bus is also on demand on Thursday and operates around the island from 7am until 7pm. Call in advance on 01856 821360. The Sanday Bus meets the ferry daily from May 2 until September 27 and will drop off and pick up at any roadside location. Ring 01857 600344 or 07513 084 777 before 6pm the previous day. Outwith those dates, the bus is on-demand. The Westray Bus meets ferry arrivals at Rapness Pier. In winter the bus must be prebooked. Call 01857 677758 or 07789 034289.

These services are available to everyone, and Scotland-Wide Free Bus Cards are accepted for free travel. Otherwise, fares are charged at the same rate as all other bus services in Orkney, based on the distance between where users board and alight the bus (via the shortest road distance). Return fares are 1.5 times the single and children under 5 travel for free.

Ferries

Orkney Ferries operates the ferries between Mainland Orkney and 13 smaller isles. The ferry mv Hoy Head operates from Houton to Hoy and

Flotta, mv Graemsay foot ferry from Stromness to Graemsay and North Hoy, mv Shapinsay from Kirkwall Pier to Shapinsay, mv Eynhallow from Tingwall to Rousay, Egilsay and Wyre. For the North Isles the mv Earl Sigurd, mv Thorfinn and mv Varagen sail from Kirkwall Pier. The Golden Mariana runs from Pierowall in Westray to Papa Westray. You can buy tickets for Kirkwall routes at the Orkney Ferries office in Shore Street or by calling 01856 872044. For Houton departures call 01856 811397. For Tingwall departures call 01856 751360. Cars should be booked in advance and vehicles should arrive 20 minutes before the scheduled sailing time and foot passengers ten minutes before.

Planes

Flights to the North Isles are operated by Loganair from Kirkwall Airport. You can fly to Westray, Papa Westray, North Ronaldsay, Sanday, Stronsay and Eday. Passengers can take 15kg hold luggage. Bookings must be made in advance and passenger should check in 20 minutes before departure. Call Loganair on 01856 872494.

There are also several car hire firms on mainland Orkney and cars are available in the isles too, along with cycle hire.

Products

Buy from Orkney

Local production is a way of life in Orkney, with the unspoiled natural environment central to the success of many island businesses.

From outstanding food and drink products, to crafts, art, photography and jewellery inspired by the beautiful Orcadian landscape and its fascinating history, the sheer number and variety of top quality goods created in Orkney is simply staggering.

Use the links on the right hand side of the page to find out more about the range of products created and on offer right here in Orkney.

Art in Orkney

There is much to inspire the senses in Orkney. Wild, windswept coastlines, spectacular seascapes, sunrises and sunsets and long, sunny days during the summer all help draw artists to the islands.

The clear and constantly changing northern light offers a beautiful challenge to artistic people and some never give up trying to capture the island skyscape. Others are inspired by the sea crashing against the cliffs at Yesnaby, the crazily angled gables and narrow streets of Stromness, the mystical splendour of Orkney's Neolithic monuments or the flowers and birds that make the county a natural wonder.

High quality art is everywhere on the islands and there are many galleries, open studios and shops where you can buy work that depicts Orkney in some shape or form, or just captures the sense of the place. You can find out more, and even see some of our artists in action, by visiting the Orkney Crafts Association website.

All kinds of media and art forms are explored here, from large oils and small watercolours, to landscapes woven in wool or felt, and to sculptures in wood, metal, ceramics or glass. Fine art cards and prints are an affordable alternative to splashing out on an original work, though there are plenty of those to choose from too. Watch out for special exhibitions - there is almost certain to be a show open somewhere in the islands featuring local artists, visiting names or a mixture of the two. There is often an artist-in-residence at the Pier Arts Centre in Stromness. Artists will also take commissions if you have a special project in mind. Art courses are available, for a term, a holiday or a one-off workshop, specialising in many media from paint to textiles. And Orkney College runs courses too.

Not all the art in Orkney has a local theme. The Pier Arts Centre's remarkable display of 20th century art features leading lights of their day in British art, including Barbara Hepworth and Ben Nicholson, more associated with St Ives in Cornwall. Touring art shows visiting

Orkney feature works for sale and the centre has a large range of art and art books in its shop.

Craftmakers in Orkney

Orkney's heritage and landscape is an inspiration for many local craftspeople. Talented folk of all ages make an astonishing range of handmade goods in Orkney, putting new twists on some traditional skills.

Importantly, many young islanders are now following in the footsteps of their ancestors and keeping traditional Orkney skills alive. For example, Orkney chairs - with their characteristic woven straw hoods - are so popular there is a waiting list to have one made by young island craftsmen.

Just a fraction of the amazing crafts you can buy in Orkney include: jewellery, pottery, ceramics, tapestry, textiles, knitwear, sculpture, carved stone and wood, musical instruments, stained glass, home furnishings and furniture. Materials used vary from the wool of local sheep to recycled items found on the beach. Many, but not all, of the craft outlets and studios in Orkney are featured in Orkney Crafts Association's Craft Trail. There is a handy booklet with addresses, maps and details about all the members and their locations are signposted on the roads.

You can find many craft items in the independent shops that Orkney is famous for. And you may find interesting wares at special exhibitions throughout the year. Many of the artisans have websites for mail ordering goods and some travel to major craft fairs and exhibitions to show the rest of Britain the high quality of Orkney craftsmanship. The Orkney Craft Association website is a good place to start when looking for goods produced in the islands.

Orkney's Food and Drink

Orkney is a food lover's paradise, where the pristine environment produces a bounty of delights. The green, fertile fields and clean, clear seas help local producers create much sought after goods.

The islands are full of small-scale artisan producers who are always happy to tell you exactly where your food has come from. Many are members of the local group Orkney Food and Drink, which helps bring them together and promote the products to a wider audience

Meat from cattle and sheep raised on Orkney's lush green fields enjoys protected European status and is highly prized throughout the UK. For a uniquely delicious flavour you can sample the hogget or mutton from North Ronaldsay lamb, a hardy ancient breed that feeds almost exclusively on seaweed. There's even a herd of water buffalo in the islands, with the rich and healthy meat produced by Orkney Buffalo proving increasingly popular. Orkney's butchers are also well versed in using local meats to create a range of prize winning produce, including sausages, black pudding, haggis and pies. Four local butchers work together to ensure the islands abbatoir is kept in use so local meat is available to local buyers.

Our clean seas offer a sustainably managed harvest of salmon, hand-dived scallops, crab, lobster and spoots (razorfish). Salt and air dried fish - the traditional way of preserving fish in the islands - is another speciality widely available, as is soused herring, smoked white fish and kippers.

Orkney's lush grass, which grows in pastures near the sea, provides a natural stress-free environment for dairy cows. And stress-free cows mean good milk and dairy products - Orkney Cheddar and Orkney Ice Cream are the most notable - created with great care using traditional processes.

You might think vegetables have a tough time growing so far north, but Orkney is actually the perfect place for producing quality potatoes, other roots and leafy greens. Growers also use polytunnels to grow succulent strawberries and ripen tomatoes during the long summer days.

Our bakers produce a scrumptious range of homebakes, biscuits, fancies, breads, rolls and the unique bere bannock - a thick scone of primitive barley grown and milled in Orkney and baked on a girdle (iron). Try one served with Orkney farmhouse cheese. Other favourites are oatcakes and Orkney fudge.

Restaurant specialities in Orkney include breadcrumbed and fried Grimbister Cheese as a starter, or plain and simple partan toes (crab claws). Orkney beef or seafood must top the list for main courses, and Orkney fudge cheesecake is the sweetest of all desserts. Orkney is also famed for its huge number of cafes and tradition of tearooms, in town and country.

There are two whisky distilleries in Orkney – Highland Park and Scapa - with the former's spirit voted the best in the world. Orkney's two breweries – the Highland Brewing Company at Swannay Brewery near Evie and the Orkney Brewery in Quoyloo, brew award-winning cask and bottled ales. Meanwhile, the Orkney Wine Company - the UK's most northerly winery - produces a fabulous variety of traditional fruit wines and liqueurs, and Orkney Distilling makes Kirkjuvagr Orkney gin and is set to open a distillery in Kirkwall in 2017.

You can find out much more about Orkney's food and drink producers by visiting the Orkney Food and Drink website and watching the short film below. For your own guide to where to find the very best food and drink, download a copy of the Orkney Foodies Guide 2015/16.

Jewellery in Orkney

Orkney has the largest concentration of craft jewellers in Scotland and their work is exported around the world. The local industry continues to grow as established firms are joined by new producers, inspired by the Orcadian landscape.

Orkney jeweller, Ola Gorie, led the way for heritage jewellery and was the first to make handmade jewellery here since Viking times. She was inspired by Norse art, such as the Maeshowe dragon, carvings in St Magnus Cathedral and a brooch found in an ancient grave in Westness, Rousay.

Now Orkney is famous for its many talented craft jewellers who draw on Orkney's culture and natural beauty for their designs. Stunning contemporary pieces are also created in the many workshops where you can often call in and see the craftspeople at work.

Many of the jewellery brands you see in Orkney are big names in the high streets of the south: Sheila Fleet and Aurora both have outlets outwith Orkney. And one of the most famous names in local jewellery, Ortak, has been revived and relaunched after going into administration in 2013.

When you witness the sheer craftsmanship and attention to detail that goes into the work by small teams of people in Orkney you realise how special some of these pieces are and how passionate the artisans are about their handcrafted products. Their work is completely different from the mass-produced pieces of jewellery made in factories across the world. Most jewellers welcome visitors to watch them work and will undertake commissions and design one-off pieces. If you can't get out to a workshop, you will find work by Orkney's craft jewellers in shops in the towns and around the isles. Most jewellers and silversmiths also have their own websites and offer mail order services.

Photography in Orkney

Orkney is the perfect location for a photographer - professional or amateur. It has some of the best locations and scenery for people to practice their skills.

Photography has been a popular profession and hobby in Orkney for a long time - highlighted by the range of books available locally which feature archive collections. And today, photography for all events and occasions is well served in Orkney by professionals who are ready to capture your moment forever

While many local artists have chosen photographic work as their main medium, and you can find beautifully artistic photographs throughout the islands, family events from weddings and christenings to anniversaries and graduations are also well catered for.

Family portraits, celebrating the birth of a baby and passport photographs can be easily arranged. Corporate photography for publicity, advertising, websites or in-house magazines is covered, as are the recording of news and community events. You can hire a photographer to take images for your book or buy a book created by a photographer.

Services from picture repairs to printing to enhancement of your own photographs can all be done for you without leaving Orkney. Calendars, postcards, framed prints and posters featuring Orkney's stunning coastal and landscape images can be bought off the shelf.

Nature and Wildlife

With its mild climate, fertile green land and stunning coastline, Orkney is a paradise for nature lovers all year round.

Every season has its own charm and beauty, from the endless days of summer with seabirds clamouring on the cliffs, to the short days of winter when the land is free of visitors and you can enjoy the quietness and rugged beauty of our coastline.

Unique animals live here, including the Orkney vole, while rare plants thrive in the pollution-free air. A pair of Sea Eagles are attempting to make Hoy their home, and sealife is abundant.

Nature is all around you in Orkney. View our film and explore our seperate sections below to get inspired.

Animals in Orkney

Orkney is a wonderful place to spot wildlife and is home to some very rare species of animals.

Among them is the Orkney vole (Microtus orcadensis) which is a unique sub species of the European vole, not found in mainland Britain. These are larger than the field and bank voles found in the rest of the country. You can spot the voles' runs on coastal grassland and might be lucky enough to see one. Short-eared owls and hen harriers hunt them for food. This small rodent even has distinct sub species between different Orkney islands with varying head sizes. Foxes and deer, which were brought to Orkney by ancient people for hunting, and badger are now extinct in Orkney.

Brown hare are common and can often be seen running across farmland. Mountain hare live in the hills and moors of Hoy and are brown in summer and white in winter. They were reintroduced in the 18th century. Rabbits also abound. One of Britain's most elusive animals, the Eurasian otter, is alive and well in Orkney. But despite an otter crossing road sign in Kirkwall near the Peedie Sea, you need plenty of patience to sit still to see one of these shy creatures near sheltered coasts, rock pools and lochs. Look for their droppings or spaints or the marks of webbed feet and make your search at dawn or dusk. Other mammals include long-tailed fieldmice, pygmy shrews and hedgehogs.

Orkney is also home to many species of insects including butterflies, moths and the dreaded midges and is one of the last habitats of the endangered great yellow bumblebee.

Important birds on the reserves include the hen harrier, short-eared owl, kestrel, rare corncrake, snipe, oyster-catcher, curlew, red-throated diver, lapwing and many species of wild duck and geese.

Orkney has 36 Sites of Special Scientific Interest and 13 Special Protection Areas which are important areas for wildlife protected by Scottish Natural Heritage and 13 reserves managed by the RSPB. Wildlife projects are also managed by many other organisations in Orkney including the Scottish Wildlife Trust, the Farming and Wildlife Advisory Group, Orkney Field Club and Orkney Islands Council.

Birds

The RSPB looks after 13 nature reserves across Orkney, so it's clear the islands are a very important area for birds. Large numbers pass through in spring and autumn on migration, with a number of rare breeds often making an appearance.

Orkney's cliffs are home to vast numbers of breeding seabirds during the summer, with Marwick Head and Mull Head on the mainland, and Noup Head in Westray, popular sites for seabird spotting. If you're looking for puffins, many of Orkney's huge population are on the inaccessible Sule Skerry, but there are plenty of spots around the islands to catch a glimpse of these charming birds, particularly the Castle o' Burrian in Westray and Marwick Head on the west mainland.

Waders breed in Orkney's wetlands and can also be found in the lochans on the moors of the mainland, Rousay and Hoy. The moors are also the place to see hen harriers and short eared owls.

In winter, you'll find a huge variety of wildfowl on the freshwater lochs and in sheltered sea areas, and in spring you'll see the ducks in their finest plumage.

Fulmars

The fulmar is known as a mallimack or malli in Orkney dialect. Its common names are the Northern fulmar, fulmar petrel or Arctic fulmar and its proper name is Fulmarus glacialis. Orkney is a paradise for seeing seabirds but don't get too close to these relatives of the albatross. They repel predators by regurgitating foul oil from their stomachs and can accurately squirt you from three feet to defend their nests. The substance is also used to feed chicks. Fulmar oil was used to light lamps in times past in the Hebridean island of St Kilda and even to pay rent to the laird. Fulmars only arrived in Orkney a century or so ago but there are now 91,000 pairs here.

The fulmar can be seen on cliff ledges across Orkney with Marwick Head, near Birsay and The Noup on Westray being good spots. Half of all the pairs can be found on the cliffs in Hoy and you'll see them if you take the walk to the Old Man. The bird looks gull-like but has tubular nostrils and grey wings which it glides with stiffly and flies with short beats. The head and underparts are white, the back, wings and tail grey. Its span is 45-50cm and wingspan 102-112cm. Pairs are monogamous and return to the same nest site each year. The fulmar feeds on plankton and discarded offal from fishing boats. They only lay one egg but can live for up to 40 years.

Since the 1950s a research project into fulmar breeding has been carried out on the uninhabited Orkney isle of Eynhallow by Aberdeen University. This involves weighing chicks and monitoring numbers.

Guillemots

The guillemot (Uria aalge), known as the aak in Orkney, has a dark brown head, neck and upperparts. It has a distinctive white line across closed wings. The bill is black and tapering and legs are dark blue. The guillemot's eggs are pear shaped to prevent them rolling off cliff ledges. There are around 181,000 adults in Orkney. There are plenty of places to see them but Noup Head in Westray is always good in the summer, as is Marwick Head on the mainland. It gathers fish (sandeels) crossways in its beak, with the heads all pointing to the left or all to the right.

The black guillemot (Cepphus grille) is called the tystie in Orkney. It is smaller than the common guillemot, and can be seen on boulder beaches and low cliffs around the islands. It has smart black and white plumage and red feet and is an auk - related to the puffin and razorbill. It stays local all year round but spends winters at sea within a few miles or so of breeding grounds. The sexes are similar with a summer plumage of jet black and a large oval white patch on upper wing and under wing. In winter the tystie is whiter with a speckled grey and white back. They feed on butterfish.

They can be seen around Orkney's cliffs, especially Marwick Head, Hobbister and Papa Westray's north and east shores. The highest number of black guillemot in Britain is in Orkney and Shetland with a population in Orkney of around 5,500 adults. In England there is only one colony in Cumbria of a few pairs and 14 pairs in Wales. They are common in the Arctic and north Atlantic.

Razorbills

There are about 10,000 razorbill (Alca torda) in Orkney – a member of the auk family locally called the coulter-neb or sometimes the sea crow (sea craa). They are noisy, quarrelsome birds that nest in colonies on sea cliffs or boulders undercliff between March and the end of July. They spend winters inshore or at open sea. They are black above and white below with thick, black beaks, much blunter than the similar guillemot. The beak has a neat white line across the middle. Marwick Head in the west mainland is a favourite breeding ground as is North Hill on Papa Westray and the island of Copinsay.

Puffins

Everybody's darling, the puffin, or the tammie norrie as it is affectionately known in Orkney, brings a smile to the face of anyone lucky enough to see it. This small auk is worth seeking out in some of the hotspots in the isles where they come every year to breed between May and early August.

The best site in Orkney to see large numbers is Castle of Burrian on Westray. Here you can sit on the cliffsides for hours and watch these charming birds fly with their catch to their burrows and crevices in the cliffs. You can also get close views at the RSPB's North Hill reserve on Papa Westray and you can spot a few at Marwick Head in the west mainland, at the Old Man of Hoy, Noup Cliffs on Westray and the isle of Copinsay. There are 61,000 puffins in Orkney but 59,000 of these are on remote Sule Skerry, 40 miles west of the Orkney mainland.

The puffin is much smaller than expected on the first encounter. But though they appear clumsy on land and comical, the puffin is an expert diver and underwater flier while fishing and it flies in the air with very fast wing beats to keep itself aloft. It can hold many fish, sandeels are the favourite, in its beak, while photographers wait for that elusive shot. Just one egg is laid a year. The chick is fed frequently and leaves the nest alone around July for the sea. It will make no landfall for the first two years of its life. Outside the breeding season the puffin spends all its time at sea in the north Atlantic and North Sea. But when they land they must be the most popular bird to photograph, being snapped up for guidebooks, postcards and merchandise wherever they go

Gannets

This large, bright, attractive bird with black wingtips is known as the solan goose in Orkney. There are 5,000 pairs in Orkney with the largest colony on remote Sule Stack 40 miles west of mainland Orkney. In 2003, part of the colony moved from Sule Stack to Sule Skerry, and there are now 1,000 pairs there. In the same year, another part of the colony moved to Noup Head in Westray and there are now 600 pairs there. Given that there had been no new gannet colonies established in the North Atlantic in the twenty years up to 2003, this was an unusual occurence.

They can plunge into the sea to fish from a height of 100 feet or 30 metres and the main reason for the success of the species, while other seabird numbers are in decline, is that it eats a wide variety of fish. The gannet (Morus bassanus) always breeds in colonies on isles and inaccessible cliffs. It is while it is diving or in flight, gliding with outstretched wings or flying with deep strong wing beats that this bird is at its most spectacular, with its wingspan of 165-180cm. One of the best spots to get up close is Noup Head on Westray.

Great Skua

This great pirate of the skies is infamous in Orkney for terrorising anyone who goes near its nest during the breeding season. Always known in Orkney as the bonxie, its dive-bombing tactics around your head can be scary, although it rarely draws blood! The bonxie will harass birds to steal food and kill smaller birds. This is a problem for other species when fish stocks are scarce. Its aggressive behaviour has earned it the nickname of the pirate of the skies. It breeds on moorland, so stick to the cliffs and you are less likely to disturb them into a defensive frenzy.

A spectacular bird in flight with its dark wings with white flashes, its wingspan is 125-140cm. There are 1,700 pairs in Orkney and the second largest colony in Britain is in Hoy. However, the population has declined by 23% over the past ten years. Winter is a bonxie-free time in Orkney as it spends the season off the coasts of Spain and Africa, returning to Orkney from early April.

Wading Birds

Lapwing

Also known as a teeick in Orkney (and a peewit elsewhere in the country), these are less common than they were, possibly as a result of land drainage, but the breeding population is around 4,000 pairs. During autumn and winter, flocks of up to 500 birds are not uncommon. Many birds leave the islands under snow cover.

Redshank

The redshank is a medium-sized wading bird, which is well distributed in Orkney's marshland areas, with over 1,500 pairs throughout the islands. It has longish red legs and a long, straight bill. It is grey-brown above and whitish below. In flight, it shows very obvious white rear edges to the wings and a white 'V-shape' up its back. The winter population has been estimated at 7,000 birds.

Curlew

Also known as a whaup in Orkney, there are around 5,000 breeding pairs, with winter numbers boosted to around 20,000. The curlew is the largest European wading bird, instantly recognisable with its long down-curved bill, brown upperparts and long legs. Nationwide, there have been worrying breeding declines in many areas largely due to loss of habitat through agricultural intensification. You can spot curlews all year round in Orkney.

Snipe

Snipe have very long, straight bills that they use for probing deep into wet mud. They nest quite commonly in Orkney's wetlands and also on our wetter moors. There are probably over 3000 pairs nesting in the islands but their numbers are greatly enhanced in autumn when migrants arrive from further north. Snipe have a very distinctive display flight They dive through the air with their stiff outer tail feathers angled out from the rest of the tail. This produces a buzzing noise called 'drumming'.

Oystercatcher

This is the commonest wader in Orkney and can be seen almost everywhere except on the moors. An estimated 12,500 pairs nest in the islands drawing attention to themselves by their very noisy behaviour. On the shore, as their name suggests, oystercatchers feed on shellfish but inland, they feed largely on earthworms.

Purple sandpiper

Only a winter visitor, Orkney's population of purple sandpipers has been estimated at 5-6,000. These spend the winter on rocky seashores feeding on invertebrates. Uncertainty surrounds their migration routes, however. It is possible that their breeding grounds are on Baffin Island in Canada.

Turnstone

Another winter visitor, turnstones are rather commoner than the purple sandpipers but are often found with them feeding on rocky shores and often, as their name suggests, flicking over stones to find their food. Ringing recoveries have shown that at least some of our turnstones come to us from Ellesmere Island in the Canadian Arctic.

Birds of Prey

Hen-harrier

This is Orkney's most common bird of prey, with currently some 80 breeding females. The females outnumber males by about 3:1 and so they have a polygamous breeding system with each male having a harem of several females. While males are a pale grey colour, females and immatures are brown with a white rump and a long, barred tail which give them the name 'ringtail'. They fly with wings held in a shallow 'V', gliding low in search of food. Elsewhere in Britain, hen harriers are illegally persecuted by gamekeeping interests who claim that they take too many grouse. In Orkney we are fortunate that there is no driven grouse shooting and our hen harriers are left to breed in peace.

Short-eared owl

Also known as cattie faces, this is the only nesting owl in Orkney. Breeding pairs have been found on Eday, Hoy, the mainland, Rousay, Sanday, South Ronaldsay and Stronsay. The highest number are on the mainland and they are regularly seen around the airport in Tankerness. You won't see them much in mid-winter (because they become more nocturnal) but they start to show around February through till October. Probably about 50 pairs nest in the islands. Their main prey is the Orkney vole, this small mammal making up as much as 90% of the food of many of our owls.

Sea Eagle

It was confirmed in April 2015 that a pair of juvenile Sea Eagles were attempting to nest in the Orkney island of Hoy. The two birds, which have been regular visitors to the island in recent years, have built an eyrie above the Dwarfie Stane, near Rackwick. According to the RSPB, the nesting attempt could fail, but the pair are being monitored carefully. Sea eagles are the UK's largest birds of prey with a wingspan of almost two-and-a-half metres. A re-introduction programme began in the late 1960s on Scotland's west coast and islands, before being expanded to the east coast. It's thought Orkney's two birds could have arrived from Scandinavia. Anyone keen to see them is asked to stay in the roadside car park, instead of heading down to the Dwarfie Stane itself, to minimise any disruption to the pair.

Migrating Ducks
Shelduck
A mainly black and white duck with a conspicuous chestnut breast band; larger than a mallard but smaller than geese such as greylag and Canada. It has a particularly prominent red bill, black-green head, and chestnut and white upperparts. In flight, shelducks look heavy and have slow-beating wings. Having been away to the coast of Germany where they moult, they begin to return to Orkney in mid-winter with numbers building through till May. The majority of breeding birds have left by August.

Teal
Breeding pairs are found throughout the islands with the highest numbers reported from Shapinsay with a peak count of 2,650. Teals are small dabbling ducks. Males have chestnut coloured heads with

broad green eye-patches, a spotted chest, grey flanks and a black edged yellow tail. Females are mottled brown. Both show bright green wing patches in flight.

Mallard

Widespread throughout the islands, the mallard is a large and heavy looking duck. It has a long body and a long and broad bill. The male has a dark green head, a yellow bill, is mainly purple-brown on the breast and grey on the body. The female is mainly brown with an orange bill.

Wigeon

Only small numbers of this beautiful duck nest in Orkney, possibly as few as 50 pairs but it is our commonest duck species in winter with probably over 30,000 wintering in the islands. The males have red-brown heads and necks with a yellow forehead and large white shoulder patches in the wings. The females are much duller, as in all ducks, but are distinguished by a large pale area on their underparts.

Shoveler

The male is another spectacularly lovely duck but both sexes share one special feature – their large, spatulate bills which they sweep through soft mud and vegetation when they feed. Perhaps 150 pairs nest in Orkney making the islands one of the most important places in Britain for this species.

Pintail

This is perhaps the most graceful of our ducks, their long slender necks being almost swan-like. The drake is particularly lovely with a chocolate-brown head and neck with a delicate white stripe. Only about 30 pairs of pintails nest in the whole of Britain and Orkney holds about half of them.

Tufted duck

A medium-sized diving duck, smaller than a mallard. It is black on the head, neck, breast and back and white on the sides. It has a small crest and a yellow eye. In flight it shows an obvious white stripe across the back of the wing. This is a common breeding species in Orkney with wintering numbers building in September and declining again in March.

Eider duck

The UK's heaviest duck, and its fastest flying. It is a true sea duck, rarely found away from coasts where its dependence on coastal molluscs for food has brought it into conflict with mussel farmers elsewhere in Scotland. Eiders are highly gregarious and usually stay close inshore, riding the swell in a sandy bay or strung out in long lines out beyond the breaking waves. They are widespread in Orkney as a breeding species, particular on uninhabited islands and holms. They are known locally as 'dunters'. After they have mated with their females, the males take no more part in the breeding cycle and gather in large flocks to moult.

Longtailed duck

The long-tailed duck is a small, neat sea duck that is mainly a winter visitor to Orkney. They have small round heads and steep foreheads. In winter, the male is mainly white with some brownish-black markings. He also has greatly elongated tails feathers - hence the name. Females are browner. In flights, they show all dark wings and white bellies. They are recorded throughout the year in Orkney but usually only 1 or 2 birds are present in mid-summer. The first returning birds arrive in September and October and the majority have left by the end of May. The Orkney name is 'calloo' which refers to the beautiful echoing call that they can be heard to make on calm days.

Goldeneye

A medium sized diving duck, found on both fresh and salt water, the largest numbers can be found on Harray and Stenness lochs and around Scapa Flow. Males look black and white with a greenish black head and a circular white patch in front of the yellow eye. Females are smaller, and are mottled grey with a chocolate brown head. In flight, the birds show a large area of white on the inner wing. Although small numbers of goldeneyes nest in Scotland, they are woodland ducks (breeding in holes in trees) and no such habitat exists here to encourage them to nest.

Orkney's climate

As well as the 'four seasons in one day' saying, many folk describe Orkney as having only two seasons a year! Long, bright days in the summer, and short, dark days in the winter. But there is a lot more to our weather than that...

As most local residents will know, Orkney weather can be very changeable, very quickly. Mornings that start sunny and still can develop with a cold wind or even hail storms and heavy rain. But change is a constant here and wind blows away showers more quickly than in other regions.

The two seasons a year adage relates to the light season in the summer when in June the skies barely get dark, while in winter there are short hours of daylight. Because of the influence of the Gulf Stream, the Orkney climate is very mild compared with places on the same latitude, such as Russia or northern Canada. Snow and frosts that hit mainland Britain are seldom present in Orkney. An occasional light sprinkling of powder on the Hoy Hills just adds to the picturesque view. There is only a 10 degree Celsius difference between the summer average temperature of 15C and the winter of 5C.

Winters are on the wet side and strong winds and gales are frequent. The wind is quieter in the summer but a breeze is almost always a feature - good news as it keeps midges away! Occasionally in the summer, fog or sea-haar will linger round the coast, mainly in the east, while the west may be basking in sunshine.

Nowhere can beat Orkney's magical skies and landscape on a fine day. Its beauty is undiminished by air pollution and the quality of the clear northern light is a magnet to artists. On a fine night, spectacular aurora borealis displays take the breath away.

Coast

Orkney's stunning coastline has a rich variety of habitats - from the high red sandstone cliffs of Hoy to the sheltered beaches of Sanday, the gentle shoreline of Scapa Flow to the storm-battered, rugged coast of West Mainland.

These habitats include maritime heathland and salt marsh, which are home to many species of maritime plants. It also supports world renowned fauna and flora, offering prime locations to see rare seabirds, hunt for lucky cowrie shells (groatie buckies in Orcadian) or spot the Scottish primrose (Primula scotica).

Geological features include sea stacks, such as the Castle o' Burrian, Westray or the world-famous Old Man of Hoy standing 140 metres high, which are popular with climbers. Chris Bonnington climbed the Old Man in 1966 and again in 2014. Geos, such as Sand Geo, Marwick Bay and Skipi Geo, Birsay, are narrow long slots carved along fault lines by the sea. And gloups or blowholes such as The Gloup in Deerness are spectacular in a storm as the sea cascades up like a fountain. Yesnaby in Sandwick is a dramatic place to view inlets, sea stacks, gloups and geos. In Stronsay you can see the natural arch called the Vat of Kirbister. There are fossils in the cliffs at Yesnaby too but to guarantee seeing those head for the Fossil and Heritage Centre in Burray. Natural flagstone, used for roofs, can be found in Westray. There is a permanent exhibition about flagstone at Westray Heritage Centre which also has a model geo. The tidal island of the Brough of Birsay can be visited at low tide when you can explore the rock pools as you cross the causeway and find crabs and anemones.

Manmade features on the coast include the extensive wartime lookouts and batteries around Scapa Flow, fishermen's huts at

Marwick Bay and nousts at Birsay where boats were hauled up into hollows above the storm beach. Remains of Iron Age brochs can be found near the coast including on Rousay, Hoy and the Broch of Gurness at Aikerness.

Family beaches for fun days out building sandcastles or taking a swim can be found across the islands, including at Scapa Beach, near Kirkwall, Dingieshowe Beach in Deerness and at Cata Sand with its spectacular dunes in Sanday

Flora

Wildflowers carpet the cliff tops, wetland, heaths and even roadside verges in Orkney with a colourful display from April to September. There are 500 native plants and 200 more that have been introduced, making Orkney a flower-lovers haven.

Many come here to see one of Britain's rarest flowers, the Scottish primrose (primula scotica) which is only found in Orkney, Sutherland and Caithness. Orkney sites for this small plant with deep purple flowers include Yesnaby, the west coasts of Rousay and Westray, North Hill on Papa Westray and South Walls. It flowers in May and July.

Sea cliffs are covered in the pink haze of sea pink or thrift in the spring, along with sea campion, spring squill, bird's foot trefoil (known as cocks and hens in Orkney), eye bright, wild thyme, grass of Parnassus and ox-eye daisies. Ten per cent of the UK's maritime grasses can be found in Orkney and include marram grass and lyme grass. And in bogs you can find sphagnum moss. Marshland and moorland are the places to see rare orchids including the red Northern marsh orchid, the early marsh orchid, the heath orchid and frog orchid. Oyster plants grow near the shore.

The clean air of Orkney supports many types of lichen. Ling and bell heather carpet moorland in Hoy and Rousay, sprinkled with patches of cotton grass. Wet areas provide habitat for insect-eating plants, the common and great sundews and butterwort.

Woodland plants thrive in Orkney in Berriedale Wood, an important native wood on Hoy. Here grow rowan, hazel, birch and aspen. In Binscarth Woods near Finstown, Balfour Castle on Shapinsay and at Woodwick in Evie, the woodland floor shimmers purple when the bluebells flower in May. The trees provide a home to the sparrowhawk.

On roadside verges and unsprayed fields you will find fat hen, celandines and primroses. Clouds of yellow gorse brighten up coastal areas and angelica grows wild.

Schoolchildren in Orkney have planted many species of locally grown wildflower seeds including vetches, red clover, red campion and knapweed to encourage bees.

A number of private gardens have been opened to the public in recent years for the Orkney Garden Trail, helping to raise funds for charity. Find out more from our link on the right hand side of the page.

Sealife

Orkney's abundant sealife makes the islands a wildlife lover's paradise.
Porpoises, dolphins and whales are regularly seen around the coast, with basking shark sightings on the increase too.

Seals, or selkies as they're known locally, are everywhere and you're guaranteed to see some lounging on skerries at low tide or swimming near the shore. Selkies often feature in Orkney folk tales, which regularly involve them shedding their skins and taking human form.

On the shore, exploring the rockpools is an exciting activity for all ages - you'll find mussels, crabs, sea urchins, anenomes and starfish in the clear water, and limpets and barnacles clinging to the rocks.

Explore our rich sealife within each section below.

Porpoise

Harbour porpoises are frequently seen all year round the coast of Orkney. This is the smallest cetacean in Orkney waters, measuring up to 1.8m in length. It is shy of revealing much of its body above water. You need to watch the surface of the sea closely for a glimpse of its back and small fin as harbour porpoises rarely leap clear of the water. It is related to the dolphin and can be distinguished by its small triangular fin, rather than the dolphin's sickle-shaped fin. The harbour porpoise travels alone or in groups but up to 100 have been spotted coming together for an abundant food supply of fish.

Sightings of harbour porpoises have been made from the shore in Orkney including Hoxa Sound on South Ronaldsay, Rackwick on Hoy, Cantick Head on Hoy, and from Tankerness in the east mainland. But they may be spotted anywhere from the coast or while sailing on a ferry between the isles or across the Pentland Firth and frequently in Scapa Flow.

The Sea Watch Foundation lists recent sightings in Orkney on its website and welcomes reports of sightings from anyone, anytime. It holds regular annual whale and dolphin watch surveys in Orkney when the public can join experienced observers.

Dolphins

Playful dolphins are a popular attraction and several species can be spotted passing through Orkney in the summer months. These include Risso's dolphin, the Atlantic white-sided dolphin, white-beaked dolphins and the common dolphin. Dolphins have just one calf after a ten or 11 month pregnancy, depending on the species

The white-beaked dolphin (Lagenorhynchus albirostris) is one of the most commonly seen dolphins around Orkney. It grows to around 2.5-2.7 metres at adulthood. It is characterised by its short thick creamy-white beak and curved dorsal fin. White-beaked dolphins are acrobatic and social animals which frequently ride on the bow wave of high-speed boats and jump clear of the sea's surface. The dolphin may easily be misidentified as the Atlantic white-sided dolphin, although the white-beaked is more common here. The white-beaked dolphin is also typically larger, and does not have yellow streaks on its side.

The Atlantic white-sided dolphin is common offshore in deep Atlantic waters around Scandinavian and Nordic countries, Orkney, Shetland and the north of Scotland. On the small side, at up to 2.8m, it has a sloping head and short thick beak. It has a large sickle-shaped dorsal fin. They often breach and sometimes bow-ride. Uniquely amongst dolphins it has a yellow patch behind its dorsal fin.

Risso's dolphin has frequently been seen around Orkney. Larger than the white-beaked dolphin, at up to 3.8m in length, it has a tall sickle-shaped fin, a blunt rounded head and no beak. This type of dolphin is distributed from Orkney down to the Mediterranean in small numbers and visits here between May and September. It is the kind used in marine parks for displays. Recent sightings include Eynhallow, Birsay and South Ronaldsay.

The short-beaked common dolphin is one of the most playful and often breaches. It is found in the Atlantic off Orkney and Scotland with sightings all year round but mostly between July and October. Seen recently in Hoxa Sound between South Ronaldsay and Flotta, it is up to 2.6m long, has a long slender beak, sometimes tipped white and a distinctive hourglass pattern of tan on lower flanks with a grey back. It lives in large groups.

The bottlenose dolphin is extremely rare in Orkney but it has been sighted recently east of the island of Shapinsay.

Whales

There is always great excitement in Orkney when a pod of killer whales or orcas is spotted. This happens several times most years - in fact 90 per cent of sightings of orca in the UK are off Orkney and Shetland. This large member of the dolphin family can measure up to 9.75m in length. It is easy to recognise by its distinctive black and white livery. This awe-inspiring predator lives in social groups called pods with the oldest female in charge. Pods with up to 150 animals have been spotted east of Orkney. They mainly hunt for fish including herring and mackerel but also snatch seals and porpoises, often seen throwing their prey up in the air. The best time to see them around Orkney is between May and September although they are present year round. Sightings include Sanday, North Ronaldsay, Yesnaby and mid Pentland Firth.

The most common baleen whale around Orkney, which has plates and sieve-like hairs, rather than teeth, is the minke whale. These whales measure up to 8.5m and are slender with a central ridge and a small dorsal fin. Hotspots to see them are the coastal waters around headlands, islands and in channels. Sightings recorded include from Hoxa Head, Marwick Head, St Mary's Pier and Birsay Bay.

Other whales which are much rarer but have been Orkney visitors include the pilot whale, sperm whale, humpback whale, fin whale, sei whale, and blue whale. A fifty foot sperm whale sparked local interest in October 2011 when it appeared in shallow water near Kirkwall Pier. It remained there for some time before heading out to deeper water.

In days gone past a whale stranding was a cause of celebration as it meant a large source of food, oil and bone. Whales were driven ashore in earlier times. Many Orcadians joined the whale fishing fleets to Iceland and Greenland in the 18th and 19th centuries and later to the Antarctic. Now the appearance of the whale is heralded as a good thing for eco tourism, rather than food. Displays in the Stromness Museum tell the story of Orcadian whalers and show artefacts, such as scrimshaw, which is carved and elaborately engraved whale ivory.

Seals

Orkney is an internationally important breeding site for two species of seals – the grey and the common seal. These charismatic creatures are both friendly and inquisitive, but it's best to steer clear of mothers with pups. You are certain to spot seals here basking on skerries at low tide, or even have them follow you in the water as you walk along the shore. If you whistle or sing it helps with the Pied Piper effect. Both grey and common seals make their home in Orkney.

Grey seals are the heavier of the two and give birth to their milky white pups from October onwards. The pups remain on land to suckle for 18-21 days to put on fat for the cold winter at sea. They have a Roman nose and females live for about 35 years and males for 25. Fifteen per cent of the world population of grey seals are in Orkney. There were about 25,000 in Orkney in 2007. They favour isolated skerries and beaches and can be seen spread out from one another while basking.

Common seals are less common than grey seals. They are smaller and have their pups around June and July. These pups can go to sea almost immediately. This species spends days at sea feeding but there are plenty of haul-out areas to spot them on when they come ashore. Just listen out for their mournful, haunting cry. Females live for about 30 years and males for 20.

The number of common seals has declined in Orkney by around 50% in the past ten years, and no one is certain what has caused this. Presently, there are about 7,000 common seals here.

Orkney folk legends tell of the magical race of selkies – seals in Orcadian dialect. It is said they shed their sealskins on Midsummer's Eve, and became beautiful seal folk who bewitched humans.

Basking Sharks

Don't rush out of the water or off the beach if you see a gigantic shark moving slowly near the coast with its giant mouth open. It is most likely a basking shark which is huge but harmless. This is the largest fish in British waters and it can be seen near the coastline in Orkney. It is rare to catch a glimpse, but if you do, it's an awesome sight. It can weigh around 17 tons and the largest recorded in the world was more than 12m long. They are usually 6-8m long and are a typical shark shape with a large dorsal fin. They are plankton and small invertebrate filter feeders. They typically move slowly with mouth open, filtering huge volumes of water to get food. In the winter they dive to great depths to get plankton while in the summer they are mostly near the surface, where they appear to be basking. Hotspots for basking shark sightings include Eynhallow and off the Old Man of Hoy.

One of Orkney's greatest mysteries is the story of the Stronsay Beast. In 1808 a dead monster was found decomposing on the rocks on Stronsay. The giant creature was longer than an average basking shark and appeared to be serpent-like, which may have been due to the decomposition. The creature had rotted away before zoologists of the day could do a thorough examination and descriptions matched no species they knew about. Work to try and identify it is ongoing from a small sample that survived and from recorded eye witness accounts. There is a strong possibility that the monster was a basking shark, according to Orcadian-born geneticist Dr Yvonne Simpson.

Seasons in Orkney

Although it's often said that you can experience all four seasons in a single day in Orkney, there are still clear distinctions as the months pass by. From the appearance of lambs and cows in the fields during Spring and the long, hazy days of Summer, to the harvest of Autumn and the wild and invigorating Winter, Orkney has a season for every mood.

Orkney Spring

Spring in Orkney is a magical time when wildflowers carpet the islands and the days lengthen after the long winter. The month of May has the second highest average hours of sunshine of the year, after August. Lambs are born and skip around the fields and cattle taste their first fresh grass as they are turned out after a winter in a warm byre. Seabirds arrive in their thousands to nest on the cliff ledges. In fact spring is a great time for humans to visit too while there are plenty of beds to be had, before the festivals and summer events lure the bulk of visitors to the islands. And Orkney's fantastic ancient monuments and attractions are that bit quieter too.

Beware though in late March when equinoxal gales can hit the islands, bringing a dramatic element to the scene, making a walk down the street an adventure in the wind. But even the April showers here can have a good side to them, for this is the time for brilliant rainbows, casting their arcs of colour high in the sky which can be seen for miles. By sunny May you have good chances of enjoying more peaceful times sitting by harbour sides and on garden benches watching the world go by. And even if the day starts unpromisingly, the weather can change to glorious sunshine and often does.

On 17 May Orcadians celebrate ancient Norse connections by marking Norwegian Constitution Day with visiting friends from Norway with a parade, concert and dance. And at the end of May the air will be alive to the sound of many fiddles as the Orkney Folk Festival gets underway in venues across the county.

Orkney Summer

If you are not used to the early dawn of an Orkney summer's day, you may waken very early. In high summer in June there is almost continual daylight. Orkney's latitude at 59 degrees north means the sun is above the horizon for 18 hours. It rises at around 4am and sets at about 10.30pm. But it is still twilight for much of the night as the sun only dips just below the horizon. This period of not-quite darkness is known in Orkney as the 'simmer dim'. You can celebrate the summer solstice on June 21, the year's longest day, at the standing stone circle of the Ring of Brodgar in West Mainland. This is marked with music, poetry, readings and a tour. Folklore in Orkney tells of the Mither of the Sea, a goddess who takes up residence for the summer around Orkney, keeping the sea calm and warm.

Summer is the time when most of Orkney's festivals are staged. St Magnus Festival in June showcases music and drama and attracts international musicians. Shopping Week in Stromness in July offers week-long activities and concerts and Orkney's famous agricultural shows held across the islands in August are a chance for farmers to be recognised for their hard work in the year. You can witness the historic tradition of the Riding of the Marches, designed to keep marauders out of Kirkwall, step back in time at the Vintage Rally and witness the unique Boys' Ploughing Matches in South Ronaldsay when boys plough mini furrows on the beach and boys and girls dress up as plough horses in intricate costumes. These are popular days out for visitors and locals alike.

Those who are keen to learn more about Orkney's history, traditions and way of life can sign up for the summer school run by the UHI Centre for Nordic Studies in Kirkwall.

It's tough to fit everything in. If you'd rather have a more leisurely time of course, you could just relax and enjoy Orkney's unspoilt beaches.

Orkney Autumn

As the long bright days of summer shorten there is still plenty to inspire and lure you as Orkney moves into its autumn glory. It's not just the amazing scenery, clear air and crystal waters, archaeological wonders and stunning food. There are plenty of events and activities that only happen at this time of year which make Orkney an irresistible destination.

In September there are still two festivals to enjoy – the Orkney International Science Festival with speakers from around the globe and topics to debate and explore – and the Orkney Blues Weekend with back to back performers from other countries and parts of the UK and local bands showing off their talent. The dramatic storms of the autumn equinox are a good opportunity to experience the storm-lashed splendour of the west coast. Gorgeous sunny still days contrast with wild moments.

From October grey seals give birth to their pups, an autumn spectacle that produces around 5,000 pups a year. Fifteen per cent of the world's grey seal population make their home in Orkney. Although many of the seabirds have left these shores, winter migrants are arriving here too including geese, ducks and Whooper swans. In October you can enjoy the Orkney Storytelling Festival and listen as Orcadians have traditionally listened to tales around the peat fire. Autumn and winter are a chance to socialise and pass on stories. And even though we don't have many trees, pockets of woodland reveal their autumn colours or are enrobed with berries, while underfoot you can hunt for fungi.

As the busiest times of the farming calendar are over, parishes and isles celebrate Orkney's bounty at harvest homes and Muckle suppers. Traditional Orkney food is served and cups and prizes are handed out before a ceilidh band plays for dancing. You can experience dances unique to Orkney and even to the individual isles with an Orcadian dance partner always willing to show you the steps.

Orkney Winter

Why would you consider Orkney a good place to be in the depths of a northern winter? Simple. There are many reasons why Orkney is a great place to visit at the back end or beginning of the year with unique events and a chance to be part of the community.

December: in the lead up to Christmas there are concerts, art exhibitions and talks and lectures to attend and of course the pantomime season gets into full swing. Oh yes it does! During the first week of December a huge Christmas tree gifted by Orkney's twin region, Hordaland in Norway is lit at a ceremony marking the festival of Scandinavian St Lucy outside St Magnus Cathedral. Local schoolchildren and dignitaries parade with Norwegian guests while Kirkwall City Pipe Band plays. Inside the cathedral a tree from the forest near Grimstad in Norway is also lit.

This remembers that Grimstad was the childhood home of St Magnus and his nephew St Rognvald, who built the cathedral in Kirkwall to honour his martyred uncle. More Christmas trees are lit throughout Orkney's parishes and isles throughout the week. On midwinter's day on December 21 (and for three weeks either side) you can visit the Neolithic tomb of Maeshowe in Stenness and watch for the magical moment when light travels down the tomb's passageway to illuminate a stone inside. You can watch this on a webcam but nothing beats the near mystical experience of the real thing. On Christmas Day the unique Ba' game, a mass game of football is played through the streets of Kirkwall involving hundreds of players. There is fierce competition between the Uppies and Doonies who aim to get the ba' to their goals – the Doonies in the harbour and the Uppies opposite the Catholic church. The Boys' Ba' and the Men's Ba' are also played on New Year's Day.

On Hogmanay folk gather on the Kirk Green in Kirkwall for the bells at midnight or in Stromness at the Pierhead for the ships' whistles to sound. January and February are the quietest months in Orkney – a chance to enjoy the peace or gather for fireside storytelling and catch up with family and friends.

Explore Orkney

Seventy or so islands, 59 degrees north, nearly six hundred miles of coastline and a population of around 21,500 Orkney is a place perfect for exploring.
With bustling towns, remote islands, quiet beaches, spectacular coastline, gentle hills and green fields, you are only ever around the corner from a new experience. Find out more about our towns, islands and parishes from the links below

Kirkwall

Orkney's capital dates back to Norse times, in the 11th century, when it was called Kirkjuvagr (Church of the bay).

At that time the sea lapped at the steps of the cathedral, but now much land has been reclaimed. In 1486 Kirkwall was granted Royal Burgh status by King James III of Scotland.

The capital of Orkney has vibrant, independent shops and a lively night life in its many hotels and bars. It's also a transport hub for bus routes across mainland Orkney and the port for ferries to Aberdeen, Shetland and the North Isles. Kirkwall Airport - with links to Scotland, Shetland and, in the summer, Norway - is less than three miles from the town centre.

A Mecca for lovers of chain-free shopping, Kirkwall has everything you need, from boutique fashions, designer brands and locally designed clothing, to CDs and DVDs, jewellery, outdoor clothing, bread and cakes, linen, musical instruments, household goods and shoes. Privately owned grocery stores offer the kind of personal service that's largely disappeared elsewhere in Britain and stock local produce and international favourites. Artisan bakeries, butchers, chemists, banks and several cafes add to the exciting retail mix. The long and picturesque flagstone paved main street snakes down from the harbour, changing its name from Bridge Street to Albert Street and then to Broad Street as it goes. Kirkwall also has its own Business Improvement District scheme aimed at promoting the town centre - visit the official website for more details.

At the heart of Kirkwall stands the magnificent St Magnus Cathedral, while nearby are the Earl's and Bishop's palaces and the Orkney Museum in Tankerness House with its splendid gardens. Carrying on down narrow Victoria Street there are more shops and cafes.

On the edge of the ancient burgh there are three supermarkets and the Pickaquoy Centre with its multi-purpose arena, swimming and leisure pools, fitness and health suites, outdoor sports pitches, a café, the New Phoenix Cinema and meeting rooms. Orkney Islands Council is based in central Kirkwall at School Place. There are several venues in the town for performance including a theatre in the fantastic new Kirkwall Grammar School, community and church halls, hotel function rooms and of course, the Pickaquoy Centre. Industrial activity takes place at Hatston Industrial Estate on the edge of town and this is where you'll also find our auction mart.

Stromness

Stromness poet and author George Mackay Brown once wrote that the town's 'streets uncoiled like a sailor's rope from North to South'. Quaint closes and narrow old streets huddled between stone buildings of historical interest is the delight that is Stromness. Orkney's second largest town is an architectural gem that inspires artists and writers and is a favourite with visitors.

Those who arrive in Orkney on the ferry from Scrabster near Thurso are treated to the best view of the stone town with its piers, nousts, stores and terraces of houses, watched over by the hill of Brinkie's Brae.

Like Kirkwall, Stromness has one 'street' that meanders through the town, changing its name along the route. From the north it runs through Ferry Road, Victoria Street, Graham Place, Dundas Street, Alfred Street, Southend and Ness Road. Look out for Khyber Pass, Hellihole and Rae's Close, named after Arctic explorer Dr John Rae, on your way. You can also take an audio trip through the street, along with local voices from the past and present, with the Stromness Hometown project - download the files to begin your journey.

It may be a haven for the arty crowd and festival goers but Stromness is also a working town with useful and interesting shops and all the facilities needed to live, work and play. It is a busy diving destination with several companies offering dive charters. And increasingly Stromness is at the forefront of Orkney's pioneering renewable energy industry with the not only the European Marine Energy Centre (EMEC), but many supply chain companies and university students all based in the town; Stromness is home to Heriot Watt's Orkney campus. Stromness is where you'll find Orkney Fishermen's Society, the UK's largest crab processor, Stockan's Oatcakes and Argo's Bakery, which produces our famous Orkney Fudge.

The town has plenty of attractions, from the superb Stromness Museum to the world renowned Pier Arts Centre, and plenty of independent shops, restaurants and pubs inbetween. Stromness also plays host to the annual Orkney Folk Festival every May, when pubs and and venues are full of music and performances all weekend long. And every July the town comes alive during Stromness Shopping Week, with music, performances, charity events and lots more attracting thousands of folk every year.

Stromness maintains its maritime heritage through being the gateway to Orkney on the ferry from Scrabster, and it also has its own marina with 72 berths.

According to George Mackay Brown, the first house in the town was a hostelry on the Cairston shore which was granted a charter in 1580.

The safe harbour of Hamnavoe grew as a port and merchant town during the European wars in the 17th to 19th centuries which made the English Channel dangerous. Ships including Captain Cook's Discovery and Resolution called in 1780 and Sir John Franklin called in before his fatal journey to the Arctic.

Hudson's Bay Company ships took on men, provisions and water at Login's Well in the town in the 18th and 19th centuries and Arctic whalers from East Coast ports also took on men for the whale fishery in Greenland and Iceland. Famous inhabitants of Stromness included the painter Sir Stanley Cursiter, Isabel Gunn who joined the HBC disguised as a man and Eliza Fraser who was shipwrecked in Australia. Sir Walter Scott based several of his colourful fictional characters on Stromnessians.

East Mainland

The area east and south east of Kirkwall is cattle country, with low lying and fertile farmland. Although the East Mainland doesn't have a World Heritage Site, it does have its own nature reserve, sea caves, beaches, historical sites and attractive villages to explore

When heading east out of Kirkwall, you'll pass Orkney's airport before arriving in the parish of St Andrews. It has a well-used community hall and a vibrant school.

The area of Tankerness has good beaches for seeing seals and birds such as Arctic terns, and the Loch of Tankerness where oystercatchers, lapwings and curlews breed. The discovery of a charred hazelnut shell in 2007 in a Bronze Age mound in Tankerness was exciting evidence of Mesolithic activity in Orkney and was dated to 6820-6660 BC. You can also visit one of Orkney's most popular jewellery manufacturers in Tankerness - Sheila Fleet opened her first workshop in 1993 and now employs more than fifty people locally.

On the road to the peninsula of Deerness is Dingieshowe, a sandy isthmus where a mound is the site of a Viking parliament, known as a ting. Deerness has a shop and scattered dwellings. Newark has a fine sandy beach and small boat slipway, which can be used by non-members for a small launching fee.

Drive on to the car park at the Gloup and you can see this blowhole and walk on to the Brough of Deerness if you can brave the narrow cliff track to the site of an early monastery and chapel ruins. Carry on the spectacular cliff path and you reach Mull Head, a scenic headland crowded with seabirds in summer with its World War One gunnery range. Further on again is the Covenanters' Memorial tower erected to the memory of 200 religious prisoners who were being transported to the American colonies and lost their lives when they were shipwrecked in 1679. More tracks can be followed for a circular route back to the car park.

If you head south east from Kirkwall, you'll head towards the small harbour village of St Mary's in Holm. It has a shop and restuarant, and was once a prosperous fishing centre for the herring industry. It is now cut off from the North Sea by the Churchill Barriers, built to protect Scapa Flow during the Second World War. Across the first Barrier you can visit the iconic Italian Chapel, built by Italian prisoners of war during the conflict.

West Mainland

Orkney's West Mainland hosts a collection of some of the finest archaeological sites to be found anywhere in Europe. It's home to the Heart of Neolithic Orkney UNESCO World Heritage Site, and welcomes thousands of visitors every year.

There are the famous standing stones of Ring of Brodgar and Stenness, and the Maeshowe burial chamber. In recent years the area has continued to shed light on Orkney's Neolithic past with the ongoing excavation work at the Ness of Brodgar.

The west coast from the cliffs of Black Craig near Stromness up to the tidal historic island of the Brough of Birsay is storm-lashed and stunning with sea stacks, caves, towering cliffs, the Neolithic village of Skara Brae and a gorgeous sandy beach at Skaill Bay. A ten-mile coastal walk takes in all the sites. Sunsets viewed from here are legendary. Inland there are brown trout fishing lochs, bird reserves of moorland and marsh of international importance, Orkney's only working watermill at Barony Mills, Birsay and several village communities with shops and tearoom - serving lunches, home bakes and high teas. There are two breweries in the area, with the Orkney Brewery offering tours, food and plenty of samples! Many craftspeople have their studios in the area too.

Near the village of Orphir with its Viking church and farmstead is the ferry pier at Houton for car ferries to Lyness in Hoy. Other villages with shops and community centres are Harray, Dounby, Finstown and the more scattered communities of Evie, Rendall and Twatt. The parish of Sandwick is also spread out with farms and country houses. The two farm museums of Kirbuster and Corrigall are in the west too. Birsay has a shop, tearoom, hotel nearby and the ruins of the Earl's Palace, once the country pile of Robert Stewart, Earl of Orkney, a half brother to Mary, Queen of Scots. His son Patrick, known locally as Black Pat, added to the building. He was executed in 1615 for treason.

The Brough of Birsay can be accessed on foot via a causeway for two hours either side of low tide - tide times are posted at the site and in visitor information centres. It has traces of Pictish buildings, the remains of a Viking monastery and a lighthouse.

Burray

Burray is a small island linked to the east mainland of Orkney and South Ronaldsay by the Churchill Barriers. Once only accessible by boat, the farming and fishing community is now linked forever by the causeways.

It has a population of around 350, a new primary school, shop, hotel and harbour. Burray has beautiful sandy beaches, some of the best views across Scapa Flow and otters and seals can be seen from around the fourth barrier.

The Orkney Fossil and Heritage Centre is a fascinating place to visit. Fossils from Orkney and around the world collected by local man Leslie Firth are displayed, some up to 380 million years old, with information and illustrations. The heritage collection was started by

Leslie's father Ernest Firth, who collected everyday items from domestic and working life in Orkney throughout the 20th century including furniture, china, woodworking tools and more. There are also new displays about traditional boatbuilding in Burray and exhibits reflecting life in Orkney during the First and Second World Wars.

An Archive room has census records for Burray and South Ronaldsay from 1821 to 1901, historic photographs, various books and other documents of local interest, including original wartime manuscripts.

The shop stocks a large range of books on the subject, gemstones, jewellery and toys. The Heritage Tearoom at the Centre is run by the local community, offering tasty homemade soups, light meals, cakes and pastries, including gluten free options. The Centre opens for the 2016 summer season on the 23rd of April and closes at the end of September.

For the more adventurous types, Burray also hosts Orkney's only paintball venue, at Northfield. Also available are boat trips on Scapa Flow and clay pigeon shooting.

There is also a vibrant community spirit in Burray that has helped host a small musical festival - Glastonburray - and has seen work start on a crazy golf course and new play park in the village.

South Ronaldsay

After you cross the fourth and final Churchill Barrier, you'll arrive in the largest settlement outside Kirkwall in the east, the attractive harbour village of St Margaret's Hope in South Ronaldsay.

The village itself has everything you need - Pentland Ferries runs its catamaran ferry service to Gill's Bay near John o' Groats from 'the Hope'. There is an art gallery and craft shop, hotels, an award-winning restaurant, a golf course and the William Hourston Smiddy Museum. Films and live drama are regularly put on in the Cromarty Hall. In August the traditional Boys' Ploughing Match and Festival of the Horse is held. There are gentle sandy bays nearby at Sands o' Wright and at Herston. At Hoxa Head you can explore the remains of World War One and Two gun batteries and look across Scapa Flow to the isle of Flotta - you might even see porpoises passing by.

South of the village, as far as you can go is Burwick Pier where you can take a foot ferry to John o' Groats in the summer. You will also find the Tomb of the Eagles, a Neolithic chambered tomb which was uncovered on a farm. The family-owned visitor centre offers a welcoming talk when you can handle artefacts before making your way on a stunning coastal path to the tomb, where eagle talons were found amongst the burial. Also in the area is the recently opened

Skerries Bistro restaurant, which is situated next to the Banks Chambered Tomb.

South Ronaldsay is one of the linked South Isles, which are connected to each other by the manmade causeways, the Churchill Barriers, built by Italian prisoners-of-war during World War Two. The linked isles are Glimps Holm, Burray and Lamb Holm - home of the famous Italian Chapel, a work of art created inside two Nissen huts. The barriers have helped create beautiful beaches, especially at the third and fourth barriers.

Eday

Eday is at the centre of Orkney's North Isles and has a rich heritage and history to explore, as well as being at the forefront of research for the modern renewable energy industry.

Eight miles long, Eday is home to 150 people who are vastly outnumbered by the isle's wildlife and bird population. There is upland moor, grasslands, freshwater lochs, including Mill Loch with its bird hide and a stunning coastland with beaches of sand, flagstone and boulder and dramatic cliffs. Eday's yellow sandstone was quarried for St Magnus Cathedral and the Earl's Palace in Kirkwall. The quarry is now a habitat for fuchsia, mosses and lichen.

Routes to historic and archaeological sites are guided by the signposted Eday Heritage Walk. There are visible remains from the Neolithic, Bronze Age, Iron Age, Pictish and Norse periods. Highlights include Vinquoy Chambered Cairn and Bronze Age field boundaries and burnt mounds. The islet, the Calf of Eday, is also rich in remains.

Carrick House at Calf Sound is a 17th century laird's house which witnessed the capture of Orkney pirate John Gow who ran aground as he prepared to attack the house. It is open to visitors at certain times in the summer. At the Red House Croft Restoration project you can view a threshing mill, grain drying kilns, a forge and get refreshed at the café. Eday Heritage Centre also offers refreshments and island artefacts, working models and an insight into island life through the Eday Oral History Project recordings. In the North School nautical displays include the control room of a submarine and items salvaged from sub HMS Otter.

The island's past industries include kelp processing and peat which was sent to whisky distilleries in Scotland. The main industry now is livestock farming of sheep, cattle and small-scale chicken rearing and vegetable growing.

In recent years Eday has become the centre of the emerging tidal energy industry. The Fall of Warness, just off the island, sees marine currents race at 7.8 knots on a spring tide and is the focus of the European Marine Energy Centre's tidal test facility. EMEC offers eight test berths, connected by sub sea cables to the island. Companies including OpenHydro, Atlantis Resources Corporation and Tidal Generation Limited have all tested devices here.

There is a community co-operative shop, post office, resident nurse practitioner and school. The island also has a Gateway House, run by the Eday Partnership, which is aimed at letting people try island life before relocating permanently.

Eday has a daily ferry service and weekly flights to its London Airport. Car and bike hire is available as well as accommodation in B&Bs and a hostel.

Flotta

Flotta is an island that has changed much over the years. From its role at the very heart of Orkney's military history to the building of the Flotta Oil Terminal in the 1970s, it has always played an important part in our economy and heritage.

If you want to see Stromness and Kirkwall at the same time you need to head for Flotta in the South Isles. There are fantastic panoramic views around Scapa Flow from the island

Flotta was at the centre of the Royal Naval anchorage during two world wars and thousands of people swamped the small island. But Flotta's history goes back much further; the 8th century Flotta Stone is in the National Museum of Scotland. In 1725 the laird of Flotta Sir James Stewart murdered Captain James Moodie of Melsetter, in Kirkwall. A Flotta man, Forbie Sutherland, was a crew member of Captain Cook's Endeavour expedition and the first European man to be buried in Australia.

During World War One 10,000 troops watched a boxing match on Flotta. The battleship HMS Vanguard accidently exploded with the loss of more than 1,000 lives a mile from Flotta in July 1917. In 1915 King George V visited Flotta to inspect the troops and during World War Two, and his son George VI watched a film in the wartime cinema. Popular pipe band tune Flett of Flotta dates from shortly after this time.

All was quiet again until 1976 when the oil terminal became operational. The terminal was opened by energy minister Tony Benn. Other visitors have included Prime Minister Margaret Thatcher and the late Queen Mother. The flare atop its 223-ft stack is a landmark in Orkney. Flotta also has woodland planted first in the last world war and much added to by the terminal.

There are plenty of fascinating wartime ruins to be seen in Flotta. You can follow the Scapa Flow Landscape Partnership's Flotta Trail to see both WW1 and WW2 sites. The Peerie Museum, housed in a WW1 hydrophone hut, has artefacts of wartime and the oil industry. The island is also in the process of completing a brand new heritage centre. Wildlife includes seals and seabirds. There is self catering and a hostel and a post office. The community centre holds social events. There is also the annual Flotta 10k run, which attracts both serious and more relaxed runners to its relatively flat route.

Flotta is served by the ferry from Houton and Lyness. Oil workers mainly commute on special shuttle boats.

Hoy and Graemsay

Hoy is Orkney's second largest island and dramatically rises from the sea with mountainous moorland and glacial valleys, appearing more like a highland landscape than a typical Orkney low-lying island.

The Vikings named it High Island and Orkney's highest peak, Ward Hill reaches 1,570 feet (479 metres) and is accessible to climb. The north end of the island is the most rugged part with the cliff of St John's Head at 1,136t feet (346 metres) the highest perpendicular cliff in Britain.

Nearby is the famous sea stack the Old Man of Hoy, an iconic landmark. A scenic path recently restored, from Rackwick, a hamlet set in a dramatic bay, takes you to the Old Man. Also in the north is the Dwarfie Stane, a chambered tomb cut into rock dating from around 3,000BC. Orkney mythology tells of a giant and his wife hollowing out the rock and another tale of an evil dwarf who lived there. The area is also welcoming new visitors now because of the arrival of a pair of juvenile sea eagles above the Stane. It's believed the pair are attempting to nest at the site.

At a lonely moorland spot is the sad grave of Betty Corrigall who in the 1770s was driven to take her own life after she became pregnant. Nearly 10,000 acres of moorland and sea cliffs form the RSPB Hoy Nature Reserve. Berriedale is a sheltered valley supporting Britain's most northerly native woodland. The north end of Hoy is an ornithologists' and botanists' mecca.

This beautiful short film from local wildlife camerman Raymond Besant showcases Hoy - the high island - in all its glory.

North Ronaldsay

The island's unique seaweed eating sheep, an Old Beacon featured on prime time television and the flight path for thousands of migratory birds have all helped put North Ronaldsay on the map.

It's a small island and the most isolated and northerly of Orkney's populated isles which has preserved a distinct cultural tradition; loved by visitors and residents. It has one of the most well attended Harvest Homes anywhere in Orkney and a strong community spirit.

North Ronaldsay sheep are an ancient breed which are kept on the foreshore by a 13-mile drystone wall known as a dyke and live mainly on seaweed. They are allowed on pasture only during lambing and are managed by a sheep court of islanders. Their mutton is prized by top chefs and a mutton run, using the idea of the Beaujolais run, took carcasses to Edinburgh and London.

The Old Beacon was built in the 1780s to warn ships of the infamous rocks of Reef Dyke. It is one of the earliest lights in the country and was featured on the BBC's Restoration programme. It didn't win the top prize money but it won the Scottish heat and the project to restore it and associated buildings continues.

Nearby is the more recent Stevenson lighthouse which has guided tours through the North Ronaldsay Trust. Former lighthouse buildings have been converted into upmarket self catering units, a café and a woollen mill, using fleece from the famous sheep and selling garments and throws. The Trust also manages a modern house in the island aimed at attracting new families and keeping the school viable. It's hoped the development of more tourism attractions will create new jobs. Other facilities include a post office and the Old Kirk where island photographs and documents are displayed.

The North Ronaldsay Bird Observatory offers accommodation and the opportunity to record the fantastic array of native and migratory birds heading for Iceland, Greenland and Scandinavia. As well as a good spot for a huge number of species and rarities, North Ronaldsay has recorded pods of passing killer whales and pilot whales, as well as porpoises and dolphins - and even a walrus in 2013! A standing stone and broch and other prehistoric settlement remnants can be seen on the island.

There is a weekly car ferry from Kirkwall on Fridays and flights every day.

Papa Westray

Take the world's shortest scheduled flight and see northern Europe's oldest house on one of Orkney's smallest inhabited islands with a big community heart.

Papa Westray is one of the last places in the UK where you can experience being part of a small island community, whether you are on a brief visit or considering settling for longer.

Papay, as it is known locally, is one of the most northerly Orkney isles, just four miles by one and with a population of around 80. You can fly from Kirkwall to Westray and stay onboard for the world's shortest scheduled flight – at under two minutes in the air to Papay. You'll get a certificate afterwards. If you stay overnight your fare is vastly discounted. Papay Community Cooperative's Beltane House offers ensuite rooms or hostel dorms in converted farm cottages with self catering in two kitchens, a large lounge and dining rooms. On Saturday nights this is magically transformed into the Saturday pub with a chance of a good chat and sometimes music. Beltane is also home to a well stocked grocery shop. Nearby is the post office and craft shop. Papay is a Fairtrade island.

Other social events in sociable Papay include the Fun Weekend on the third week of July with a BBQ, ceilidh, games and sports and a carty race doon the New Hooses Brae. There is a Wednesday coffee morning and film and dance nights. Weekly services are held in the Parish Kirk and the Gospel Hall.

The Papay Development Trust is currently working on a series of projects to increase the benefits of tourism for local businesses and crafts people, and to encourage more opportunities for people to live and work in the island. A new heritage project, supported by the Coastal Communities Fund, to develop new facilities for tourists over the next couple of years will provide a boat service to take visitors to the Holm of Papay and around the island coast, a replacement minibus for island tours and will create new craft and heritage centre.

The Trust has also recruited a new Papay Ranger to lead tours and co-ordinate a programme of activities for visitors and islanders during 2015/16. For art lovers there is also the unique Gyro Nights festival every year.

Step inside the Knap of Howar and you are in a structure dating back to 3,500BC. You can access both the two rooms and then carry on along a spectacular cliff path to St Boniface Kirk, a 12th century recently restored church with a Viking hogback grave in the kirkyard. It's a simple but very atmospheric place. The northern third of Papay is the RSPB's North Hill reserve with a high population of sea birds in summer and a place to spot the rare Scottish primrose, the primula scotica. The tidal race roars where the Atlantic meets the North Sea. Around to the east side are the beautiful sheltered sandy beaches of

North and South Wick where seals will swim along as you walk the shore. St Tredwell's freshwater loch has a medieval chapel on a peninsula. At Holland House, a traditional steading in the centre of the island, surrounded by cattle grazing, you can visit the Bothy Museum with a range of farmhouse implements and fittings. Papay's calf island, Holm of Papa has sheep and prehistoric cairns.

As an alternative to flying you can take a twice weekly direct ferry from Kirkwall or a daily foot ferry from Westray in the summer. There are minibus tours and guided walks during the summer season.

Rousay, Egilsay and Wyre

Rousay, Egilsay and Wyre host some of Orkney's most magical archaeological and historical sites - with ancient brochs, cairns and tales of Vikings.

Rousay has many major archaeological delights. The coast at Westness was an important power base from the Iron Age until the 19th century. The coast from Midhowe Cairn and Broch to Westness Farm is often referred to as the most important mile of history in Scotland. Midhowe Cairn is a large stalled chambered tomb, now housed in a barn and is 5000 years old. Nearby is the Iron Age broch circular tower which still stands tall. There are also remains of Viking structures and graves. Later ruins are relics of the only wholesale example of clearances in Orkney, at Quandale and Westness by landwner George William Traill. His nephew, General Sir Frederick William Traill-Burroughs, inherited much of Rousay and built the imposing Trumland House. These days you can visit the restored gardens of the mansion.

A 13-mile road circles the island. The coastal side is fertile farmland while the lofty interior is high moorland with much of the wild parts protected. There is a large bird population of 74 species and important flora. Rushes and ferns grow in the dales. Rousay has a hotel, a bar and restaurant by the pier, a shop and post office. Yachts moor in the sheltered anchorage and there is an annual regatta and raft race. The annual Rousay Lapalso gives folk the chance to put their fitness to the test by running, walking or cycling around the island - but be warned, the hills can be tough!

Across the sound are two small islands which make up for their small size with big histories. Egilsay was an important pilgrimage destination as the site of the martyrdom of St Magnus. A 12th century church is a splendid Viking round-towered example. Here there is wetland habitat and otters can sometimes be seen as well as birds.

The isle of Wyre also has an interesting historical story. Cubbie Roo's Castle was built around 1170 as a Viking stronghold and writer Edwin

Muir spent part of his childhood on Wyre. The isle's heritage centre has historical exhibitions.

All three islands are accessed by the Ro-Ro ferry from Tingwall.

Once a year there is a public visit to the uninhabited island of Eynhallow with its ruined monastery and fantastic birdlife through the Orkney Heritage Society.

Inside

Sanday

Sanday by name and sandy by nature, the largest island of Orkney's North Isles has beautiful sandy bays and dunes, turquoise seas and a gentle, fertile landscape.

Sanday is sixteen miles long and has a population of around 550. It is a low-lying island which led to problems in the past, as ships foundered on the reefs and rocks, unable to see the shore. The first Start Point lighthouse was designed by Robert Stevenson and completed in 1807. It was rebuilt in 1870 and painted with distinctive stripes and is now a magnet for lighthouse baggers.

History lovers are drawn to Sanday too as the island has a high density of ancient and Viking structures and tombs. One of the most stunning discoveries was a Viking boat burial which contained the skeletons of an elderly woman, a younger man and a child. A rich find of grave goods included weapons, a Celtic brooch, a sickle and an elaborate and well preserved carved whalebone plaque which is on display now in the Orkney Museum in Kirkwall.

At Quoyness you can explore a Neolithic tomb and there is much else on the island. Leaflets about the archaeology are available and about wildlife, flora and shells. Seabirds, terns and wading birds are in abundance as are seals. Sanday is well known for its shells. The Sanday Ranger hosts many guided walks of special interest too. There is a new heritage centre and croft and other leisure facilities include a swimming pool, nine hole golf course and many social and special interest clubs which meet regularly. The island also has Heilsa Fjold - a youth and community centre.

A major date in the calendar is the Sanday Show in August when animals raised on the fertile land are shown and prizes awarded. The community has also organised a series of weekend events in recent years to celebrate life in the island called the Sanday Soulka.

Sanday's main settlements are Kettletoft and Lady. There are hotels, guest houses, shops, a hostel, camping, self-catering cottages and a good range of eateries. There are flights from Kirkwall six days a week or you can take the car ferry. Car and bike hire and taxis are all available, and the island also has an on-demand bus service.

Shapinsay

Shapinsay is only a 25-minute ferry ride from Kirkwall but the atmosphere of this small Orkney island can be soaked up even before you step ashore.

There is a splendid panorama of Shapinsay's attractive village, Balfour Castle and the lighthouse on Helliar Holm as you cross the channel known as the String and enter Elwick Bay.

Balfour Castle is imposing in its Scottish baronial style and is a calendar house, a Victorian novelty with 12 outside doors, 52 rooms and 365 window panes. There is also extensive woodland (for Orkney) and greenhouses which once grew peaches and figs. It was built for Colonel David Balfour the 4th laird whose farming 'improvement' in the 1840s developed agricultural land across the whole island into a grid of 10-acre squares. His pattern of field boundaries and drainage to increase cultivated areas changed the land forever. His grandfather Thomas Balfour's planned village Shoreside was renamed Balfour Village.

Balfour Castle is now an exclusive members-only hotel. By the harbour you can see David Balfour's saltwater shower with a dovecot on top, the Douche, and an imposing gateway. Up the picturesque village street is Shapinsay's Heritage Centre where you can buy crafts and artwork. Crafts including textiles, stained glass, jewellery-making, ceramics and preserves and other home industries thrive on Shapinsay. At the centre you can also learn about the history and trace family trees. William Irving, the father of Rip van Winkle author Washington Irving, was born in Shapinsay in 1740. There is a shop, post office and café, with craft producers to visit too.

There are plenty of interesting ancient sites including Burroughston Broch, excavated in 1862 by David Balfour, and the Odin's Stone. The landscape is mainly farmland after the improvements but there is a remnant of moorland and heath and the Mill Dam, now the RSPB reserve home for breeding ducks, waders, geese and swans, was created by Colonel Balfour. The Scottish Wildlife Trust's Holm of Burghlee is ungrazed maritime heathland. Low cliffs and storm beaches provide more habitat for wildlife.

Shapinsay has a thriving community school and the Shapinsay Development Trust works to create new projects and opportunities for islanders, and those keen to sample island life. Its regular ferry service helps people to stay in Shapinsay but work in Kirkwall, and there is also an Out of Hours ferry service operated by the island's Development Trust.

Stronsay

Stronsay is a beautiful island to visit and live on with magical sandy beaches backed by dunes, a stunning coastline and a main settlement with grand houses dating back to the herring fishery days.

There is a strong community spirit with the local development trust working on projects to ensure the island remains sustainable. There is a population of around 370 residents and the main centre is the village of Whitehall. Here are large houses which look more like fancy city dwellings dating from the days when the vast herring fleet came in, from the 17th century until the 1930s. Hundreds of boats would be tied up and the herring girls would travel up the east coast to Stronsay to work.

Whitehall today has a hotel, shops and a post office. The Stronsay Fish Mart Cafe and Hostel is a newly refurbished facility in the heart of the village, offering teas, coffees, homebakes, snacks, lunches and Sunday meals. The island is popular with sailors as the harbour has excellent mooring facilities. Stronsay also has a healthy living centre with a mini gym at the Junior High School as well as a swimming pool. Elsewhere, the Craftship Enterprise is a craft and gift shop offering crafting courses, days out and holidays throughout the summer season. There are excellent accommodation options in Stronsay as well as a taxi service and self-drive car hire.

Stronsay has fertile farmland and many hard-working farmers and fishermen. Local people share a community greenhouse, cutting down on food miles and providing a social place to meet and grow produce. Community groups work to provide a wide range of cultural activity, entertainment and social support.

Another part of Stronsay's history is the kelp industry which employed many Stronsay folk in the 18th century which processed seaweed for glass and soap manufacture and lined the pockets of local lairds.

Stronsay's coast has cliffs, caves, geos and long sandy beaches. Among the many coastal walks is a signed path to the Vat of Kirbister natural rock arch and gloup which is much photographed. A short walk westwards through the village brings you to the Ayre of Myers, a popular picnic spot and the first of many sandy beaches. Seals are quite often hauled out on the rocks. Rothiesholm has moorland, wind turbines and beaches. Here Bu Sands has large spaced-out dunes built from the wind-blown sand from a beach over a mile long. Some of

Orkney's rarest shells; the bubble shell (canoe) and Cyprina (coo) can be found here.

Lamb Ness and Lamb Head are home to many seabirds. Stronsay's bird reserve is one of the best sites in Europe for spotting rare migrants. A series of six information leaflets widely available cover the herring fishing industry, flowering plants, shells and seashores, birds and wildlife, archaeology, and one leaflet for children written by Stronsay children about life in the island.

The neigbouring tiny island of Papa Stronsay is the home of Transalpine Redemptive monks who offer boat rides around the island. Another small island, Auskerry has the ruined 12th century St Nicholas Chapel and a flock of North Ronaldsay sheep.

You can travel by ferry from Kirkwall to Whitehall or fly from Kirkwall airport. Find out more about visiting Stronsay using our related links section to the right hand side of the page.

Westray

Westray is known as the Queen o' the Isles and is a vibrant place to live, work and visit.

With a healthy population of 600 including 75 school age children, much of Westray's recent vitality and prosperity has been nurtured by the Westray Development Trust, formed in 1998 to buck the trend of population decline. Since then the trust has overseen many projects including a youth centre, play area, care centre, craft association, environmental projects and a community wind turbine which creates income for the islanders

Westray hit the headlines in the summer of 2009 when the carved stone figurine the Orkney Venus, known locally as the Westray Wife, was found. It is Neolithic; the oldest figure of a human found in Scotland and was discovered during the annual archaeological dig at the Links of Noltland. Westray has many other ancient archaeological sites including the Quoygrew Viking longhouse, the 12th century Cross Kirk and Viking remains at Tuquoy and St Mary's Church, Pierowall. In the Westray Heritage Centre you can see the stunning Westray Stone, a Neolithic carving and other historic treasures and search the archive. Impressive Noltland Castle is an incomplete fortress built in the 16th century by Gilbert Balfour, Mary Queen of Scots' Sheriff of Orkney. This z-plan castle is open during the day.

Wildlife lovers head for Noup Head, an RSPB reserve along high sea cliffs which is one of Britain's most important sites for sea birds, known as Seabird City, near the lighthouse. Puffins can be seen from May to August on and around the Castle o' Burrian sea stack, a former hermitage. There are many seals and cetaceans can often be seen. Salt marshes and maritime heath are a rich habitat for wildflowers.

Pierowall is the main village set on a picturesque bay and nearby Gill Pier has a marina and the ferry for Papa Westray and hosts the annual regatta. There are two general stores, arts and craft shops, a hotel, hostel, a cafe and many B&Bs in Pierowall. Elsewhere there is a gallery and cafe in the north and another general store in the south.

Westray also has a marina with seventeen berths for visiting sailors.

A car ferry from Kirkwall serves Rapness Pier daily and there are flights daily to and from Kirkwall and Papa Westray. Car and bike hire and a taxi service are available, as is a bus service connecting with the Ferry. Westray is also a Fairtrade island.

Investing

Orkney is a vibrant, energetic and forward-looking community, punching well above its weight in the world.
The pursuit of quality is a thread running through every aspect of life in Orkney. Excellence really matters here and it's also a great place to do business

Resourceful, creative and enterprising by nature, Orcadians set the bar high with whatever they turn their hand to. That's precisely why

Orkney is famed the world over for the quality of its farming, food and drink, crafts, music and art the list is long. Orcadians aim high because anything less simply wouldn't do their magnificent homeland justice.

The same ethos applies to the agencies tasked with supporting and growing Orkney's remarkably varied economy, with sustainable development and job creation the top priorities of Orkney Islands Council (OIC) and Highlands and Islands Enterprise (HIE).

Boosting inward investment is central to the vision OIC and HIE have for Orkney, with both agencies continually seeking to attract new business into the islands. The backing given to the emerging marine energy industry, through the creation of new harbour facilities at Hatston, Lyness and Stromness, and the designation of Hatston and Lyness as Enterprise Zones, is testament to this commitment.

Business Advice in Orkney

Starting, growing or moving your business can be a difficult task. If you're planning on setting up a new company in Orkney, or you're already here and you want to develop your business, there is plenty of advice on hand to help you move forward.

The first point of contact for a new or growing business is the Orkney Business Gateway office. The Business Gateway offers advice about funding, tax, finance, health and safety, environment and efficiency, IT and e-commerce, business events, networking and business contacts and also organises training courses in business start-ups and other relevant topics. Visit the Business Gateway website or call into the office at 14 Queen Street in Kirkwall for more information

While the Business Gateway caters for small and new businesses, the Kirkwall office of Highlands and Islands Enterprise provides advice and support to larger businesses and together with Orkney Islands Council's Economic Development department, provides funding and advice for ambitious businesses in a number of industry sectors. Orkney Islands Council can also advise on funding, building regulations, business rates, trading standards, planning and environmental health issues.

The local office of Skills Development Scotland can provide advice on training and education and the Scottish Agricultural College provides a support service to the agricultural industry.

Commercial Properties in Orkney

For a small place, Orkney still has plenty of space for commercial opportunities. Both Kirkwall and Stromness have designated industrial areas with food parks and quayside facilities. There are also two designated enterprise areas too, set-up to stimulate opportunities.

If you are looking to start up a business in Orkney, the local Islands Council regularly has commercial property for sale and lease.

You can also find existing businesses and commercial property for sale through local estate agents - you can find links to companies on the right hand side of this page.

Renewables Enterprise Areas
Both Hatston in Kirkwall and Lyness in Hoy are now designated enterprise areas - identified locations set up by the Scottish Government in order to stimulate manufacturing opportunities as well as investment and job creation. In support of the development of the marine renewables sector, a number of infrastructure developments have taken place at Hatston Pier, Lyness Pier, and at Coplands Dock in Stromness. Other developments to support the renewable energy sector are also planned. You can find further information on Orkney's port infrastructure from the Orkney Harbours website.

Hatston Pier's expansion provides additional berthing and working areas for the marine renewables industry where deployment of devices requires heavy lifting equipment and substantial support vessels. The extension provides a total of 385m of quay edge with 10m draft at all tides.

The shoreside development provides:

- ➤ a designated enterprise area of 10 hectares
- ➤ an ideal service base for north of Orkney tidal energy sites
- ➤ large areas of potential hard standing and warehousing
- ➤ office facilities for developers and associated businesses
- ➤ close proximity to service deployment areas
- ➤ service industries close to developers within Hatston Industrial Estate, Kirkwall

Lyness Pier, Hoy

Lyness Pier has been refurbished as a centre for the assembly, storage and servicing of marine renewable energy devices. Lyness is ideally located to offer an excellent base for R&D and deployment activities for these. The pier has been refaced and fendered giving 265 m of safe and sheltered mooring, and 4,000sq m of hard standing has been laid to assist with assembly and maintenance of marine renewables devices.

Future plans are to provide steel framed buidings, secure compounds and office and communication facilities as the site and the industry develop.

Pier and shoreside development provides:

- ➢ 260m of refurbished quay edge with up to 10m at LAT
- ➢ an ideal location for device assembly, maintenance and storage for Pentland Firth and West of Orkney
- ➢ designated enterprise areas of 7 hectares within 22 hectares of development land
- ➢ national logistics and support company on site

A number of companies are already making use of the excellent new facilities, and with designated zoning approved for shoreside development there is ample room for expansion as the marine renewables industry develops.

Get connected in Orkney

Most areas of Orkney, particularly the mainland, enjoy efficient internet provision and a new programme to bring superfast broadband to rural communities is currently being carried out.

Six thousands premises in Orkney can now access superfast broadband thanks to the Digital Scotland scheme. The aim is to have 75% of premises in Orkney connected by the end of 2016 but planning for the next phase in the project to extend reach is already underway.

Highlands and Islands Enterprise is leading on the £146m partnership investment for the area which will bring better broadband to rural communities. Funded by the Scottish Government, Broadband Delivery UK, HIE and private partners BT, the project will increase access to fibre based services from the 21% which would have seen rollout commercially to 84% of premises in the Highlands and Islands.

4G mobile internet is also now available in Kirkwall. EE has switched on the first of its 4G sites in Orkney with more set to go live during the summer of 2016. Those upgrades will see improvements outwith the town, including the north and south isles. 3G and 2G services have also been upgraded. Vodafone UK and O2 have also rolled out 4G services to customers.

Orkney's Economic Profile

Home to an enterprising and resourceful community, Orkney enjoys a very high economic activity rate.

The Orkney economy has had a traditional reliance on agriculture and fishing. However, over the last 20 years there has been a growth in employment in a number of economic sectors including manufacturing, tourism, food processing and, more recently, renewable energy.

In 2011, the population of Orkney was 21,349. This represents an increase of 10.9% since 2001 and compares to a 7.5% increase overall in the Highlands and Islands and 4.6% increase in Scotland.

According to the 2014 Orkney area profile, compiled by Highlands and Islands Enterprise, Orkney has the following characteristics:

- ➢ A business and employment base that compares closely to that of the Highlands and Islands.

- ➢ Compared with the Highlands and Islands and Scotland, a higher share of employment by industry in agriculture, forestry and fishing, construction, and transport and storage.

- ➢ Compared with the Highlands and Islands and Scotland, a higher share of employment by occupation in skilled trades and, to a lesser extent, elementary occupations.

- ➢ Unemployment rates lower than across the Highlands and Islands and Scotland. The annualised Jobseekers Allowance claimant count rate in 2013 was 1.2 per cent in Orkney, 2.4 per cent in Highlands and Islands and 3.7 per cent across Scotland.

- ➢ School attainment and school leaver positive destinations rates (i.e. not into unemployment) above the Scotland average.

- ➢ An adult qualification profile close to Highlands and Islands and Scotland profile, but with marginally more Orkney adults with no formal qualifications, but also marginally more with graduate level qualifications.

Orkney house prices have been rising in recent years, although not at the same rate as the rest of the country. The latest average house price for Orkney is £123,000, compared to £155,000 in the rest of the Highlands and Islands.

Funding and Infrastructure
Funding
The first point of contact for a new or growing business is the Orkney Business Gateway office. The Business Gateway offers advice about funding, tax, finance, health and safety, environment and efficiency, IT and e-commerce, business events, networking and business contacts and also organises training courses in business start-ups and other

relevant topics. Visit the Business Gateway website or call into the office at 14 Queen Street in Kirkwall for more information.

The local office of Skills Development Scotland provides advice on training and education and the Scottish Agricultural College provides a support service to the agricultural industry.

Grant funding is available for businesses in certain circumstances in Orkney. The first port of call for advice on what you might be eligible for is the Business Gateway office where the staff will signpost you to potential funders. You can also visit the Business Gateway website and through its Business Support Finder, you can search for organisations that give grant funding, including the Scottish Government, and you will find advice on how to apply for a grant.

Orkney Islands Council gives grant funding to local businesses through its Economic Development Fund. There are strict criteria for assistance for new business start-ups, expansions and sectoral schemes. Funding may be available of up to 30% for the construction of new buildings or the improvement of existing buildings, machinery and equipment, up to a maximum of £55,000. Expansion in areas including manufacturing for export, tourism accommodation in certain areas and the service sector if the service is not currently available in Orkney may be eligible. The council encourages business innovation and sector-wide schemes that spread the benefit across a whole sector of an industry.

Highlands and Islands Enterprise has an area office in Kirkwall and this organisation also supports business growth through funding and advice.

There are many business and community development organisations in Orkney that apply for grant funding to support community projects which generate business and growth. These groups also manage such projects on behalf of their areas, and include many isles and mainland-based development trusts and groups.

General infrastructure

- excellent schools and educational attainment levels
- further education college
- brand new hospital to be complete for 2018
- good road network
- reliable and regular air and sea links to the rest of the UK for both passenger and freight transport
- good quality housing
- superfast broadband roll out taking place during 2015

> excellent leisure facilities

Port infrastructure

An ambitious three port strategy to refurbish and build new pier and supporting infrastructure with the support of the European regional Development Fund and the Scottish Government is now complete and open for business.

Lyness in Hoy, Hatston Pier outside Kirkwall and Copland's Dock in Stromness were the 3 main components of the three port strategy along with Vessel Traffic Services software upgrades and 2 new radar sites and supporting land acquisition.

The strategy was based on the demands for additional infrastructure support for the marine renewables industry, but it is clear that the more traditional industries of oil and gas, cruise ships, and freight and supply vessels also appreciate the new infrastructure developments.

Connectivity

Six thousands premises in Orkney can now access superfast broadband thanks to the Digital Scotland scheme. The aim is to have 75% of premises in Orkney connected by the end of 2016 but planning for the next phase in the project to extend reach is already underway.

4G mobile internet is also now available in Kirkwall. EE has switched on the first of its 4G sites in Orkney with more set to go live during the summer of 2016. Those upgrades will see improvements outwith the town, including the north and south isles. 3G and 2G services have also been upgraded. Vodafone UK and O2 have also rolled out 4G services to customers.

Orkney's Main Towns

Orkney has two main towns. Kirkwall, the capital, has a population of around 9,000, while Stromness, home to much of Orkney's marine renewable energy activity, has around 3,000 people.

Both towns play an important role in Orkney's economy, housing many of our local businesses and industries, and providing home for more than half the population of the entire islands.

Kirkwall and Stromness have also been the focus of regeneration initiatives in recent years, with a new Townscape Heritage Initiative currently being run in Kirkwall.

Find out more about Kirkwall and Stromness from the links below.

Kirkwall

Kirkwall is Orkney's largest town and plays host to a wide range of shops, businesses and commercial premises. It's also the home of Orkney's main business support services, including Orkney Islands Council and Highlands and Islands Enterprise.

From its early days as a strategic Viking port to its modern role as the capital of Orkney, Kirkwall has grown to become an important business centre. On its outskirts lies Orkney's airport, Scapa Flow and its oil and inshore fisheries industry, Scotland's longest deepwater berth and numerous agricultural properties

In the thriving town itself there are a range of shops, from large national chains to small, unique and homegrown businesses.

Kirkwall is currently the focus of a five year Townscape Heritage Initiative scheme, aimed at helping regenerate the built environment in the town for the benefit of businesses and members of the public.

In recent years, the Kirkwall Business Improvement District (BID) scheme has been set up to help give town centre businesses an opportunity to directly influence developments to try and bring a new life and energy to the area. It was launched in 2013 for a five year period and has helped run a number of initiatives to attract folk to the town centre. Local businesses pay a levy from their domestic rates which is used to fund projects.

The BID team regularly hosts events in the town, including discount days and seasonal activities. Keep up to date on the Kirkwall BID Facebook page and visit the new Kirkwall BID website.

Kirkwall Townscape Heritage Initiative

Visitors to Kirkwall might have noticed a number of renovation projects taking place in and around its main streets.

The majority of the works are part of the five year Townscape Heritage Initiative scheme, aimed at helping regenerate the built environment of Kirkwall's conservation area.

The £3.5m project has been funded through the Heritage Lottery Fund, Historic Environment Scotland and Orkney Islands Council and will run until June 2019. It's a similar scheme to the Stromness THI, which came to a close in 2014. Grants are available for property owners to carry out repairs and restoration work and to bring vacant buildings back into use.

The KTHI is designed to help property owners meet the increased costs associated with carrying out repairs using historically accurate materials and techniques.

Part of the scheme will also provide training initiatives to promote skills and involvement in the care of Kirkwall's built heritage. It's hoped this will ensure a long term supply of local contractors with the ability to repair traditional stone buildings.

The aim is to regenerate the centre of the town for the benefit of local people, businesses and visitors.

A number of buildings have been identified as priorities under the scheme, including the former Carnegie Free Library on Laing Street. The new owner is going to open a retail business that will include a coffee shop, gallery and music venue. Work will start this year with an official opening scheduled for 2017.

Another important project is the restoration of the Old Storehouse on Bridge Street Wynd into a restaurant with rooms. The scheme now has planning permission and work will begin later this year. The significant investments made by local businesses will help secure the future of these two important historic buildings, as well as creating jobs for local people and providing two new attractions for Kirkwall.

The Townscape Heritage Initiative also hopes to promote more knowledge and understanding of Kirkwall's historic buildings. Two rooms at the Orkney Museum on Broad Street will be refurbished as part of the THI, creating new Medieval and Viking exhibitions to help tell the story of the evolution of the town. It's anticipated these will be ready in time for the 2017 visitor season. New digital visitor information will also be available at St Magnus Cathedral next year too. Visitors will be able to access details on their mobile devices as they walk around the building.

There have been three building grant funding rounds already - anyone still interested in improving their properties within the Kirkwall Conservation Area can find out more from Orkney Islands Council's dedicated Kirkwall THI pages or by contacting the team at:

Kirkwall THI, 15 Victoria Street, Kirkwall, KW15 1DN
Email – kthi@orkney.gov.uk
Phone – 01856 886 468

Have a look at our gallery below showcasing some of the work being carried out in Kirkwall as part of the THI scheme.

Stromness

Stromness is the largest settlement in the west mainland, and is the gateway to northern Scotland thanks to its ferry terminal linking Orkney to Scrabster. It's a busy fishing town with a strong community spirit, and a new found role at the centre of Scotland's marine energy industry.

The town's winding streets are full of character, and Stromness has long been a haven for artists and writers. It has a strong maritime heritage, with links to the Hudson's Bay Company, Arctic whaling fleets and the herring industry.

Now the town plays host to a number of wave energy developers, renewables companies and students. It's also a busy diving port, with a number of boats taking divers out to the wrecks on the seabed of Scapa Flow.

There are range of shops, cafes, hotels and arts and crafts shops in the town, and an industrial area at Garson. There is also the new Coplands Dock pier, which compliments the existing pier infrastructure. Stromness town centre and the retail sector are well represented by the Stromness Community Business Forum, which aims to promote business and community activities in the area..

Stromness was also been the focus of a successful £3.5 million Townscape Heritage Initiative (THI) which helped to restore and refurbush the historic town centre. The scheme ended in 2014 and included the repaving of the main street with local stone.

Industry sectors in Orkney

Orkney really does do the business when it comes to supporting those who run their own.

There are advice centres to help start, develop and support business, offering advice on all aspects of running a business, including help to access funding which may be available locally, and training in a range of relevant areas. Relocating here is easy with a range of services to get you on your way.

And once you are set up, there are a range of groups to represent, support or help you market your business whether it be in tourism, food and drink, energy, construction, fishing, farming or crafts.

Helping each other succeed is part of Orkney life. Explore our sectoral groups with the links below.

Agriculture in Orkney

Farming has been a way of life in Orkney for 5,000 years and remains one of the main industries in the islands.

Orkney is renowned for the quality of its produce, particularly its premium beef. In fact, Orkney has the highest density of beef cattle in Europe and is the largest dairy area north of Stirling. At the other extreme, the small flock of rare breed North Ronaldsay sheep is famous for its seaweed diet, with the meat much sought after by top chefs. There's even a herd of water buffalo in the islands.

Several agricultural organisations serve Orkney's farmers and work hard to protect the reputation and special status of the islands (Orkney Beef and Lamb both have European Protected Designation of Origin classification). Orkney Livestock Association is a farmer-led health scheme which aims to eliminate disease in cattle, while NFU Scotland is also very active locally. Orkney Farmers' Market Association supports producers through a market held in Kirkwall on the last Saturday of the month, with an enthusiastic network of local Young Farmers' clubs serving the next generation of island farmers.

Agricultural grants for farmers and landowners are available through the agricultural department of the Scottish Government, SGRPID (Scottish Government Rural Payments and Inspections Directorate) which has a Kirkwall office. Scotland's Rural College (SRUC)also has a premises in Orkney, providing skills, education and business support to the industry.

The main event in the Orkney farming calendar is the County Show, organised by Orkney Agricultural Society and held in Kirkwall's Bignold Park every August. Here, after more than a week of agricultural shows across Orkney, farmers come to show off their animals and vie for the accolade of Show Champion. Island farmers also take their animals to events in the south, including the Royal Highland Show near

Edinburgh, and regularly bring home prizes, reflecting the quality of Orkney's livestock. Local animals traditionally make very healthy prices at mart sales, both in Orkney and Aberdeen.

Many young people in Orkney continue to enter the agricultural industry, working on farms before taking on their own. Orkney College UHI offers a number of courses and qualifications to help people get the right start in the sector.

Arts and Crafts in Orkney

Orkney supports a thriving and remarkably varied crafts industry, with skilled artisans and artists producing all manner of high quality goods.

Craftspeople in Orkney can access support from the Orkney Crafts Association, which helps promote locally made products on its website and through exhibitions. The association was set up in the 1990s with help from Orkney Islands Council (OIC) and grew with assistance from both OIC and Highlands and Islands Enterprise (HIE)

A wide range of crafts and skills are represented in the Association, which counts jewellers, textile artists, knitwear designers, potters, photographers, wood turners, furniture makers, glass designers, a craft co-operative, weavers, soft furnishers, and artists and illustrators amongst its growing membership.

Members regularly join forces to market their wares at large trade and public events on the mainland, including the Country Living Christmas Fair in London and Scotland's Trade Fair in Glasgow.

In 1996 the Association set up the Orkney Craft Trail, which highlights the workshops, studios and shops of local artisans, with specially designed roadsigns and a brochure steering the public in the right direction. The Association also runs a busy crafts shop in Kirkwall during the summer months.

Other local groups offering help to craft businesses include Orkney Arts and Crafts.

Orkney has a thriving art sector as well with artists inspired by Orkney's quality of light and diverse landscapes. There are galleries throughout the islands holding regular exhibitions of new collections from individuals and groups.

Construction in Orkney

Orkney's construction industry remains in good health, with major building projects and a demand for new housing driving the sector

The Orkney Association of the Scottish Building Federation represents many of the county's construction firms, with more than 16 members operating throughout the islands. Many are experts in specialist trade skills. The federation's benefits include advice on day-to-day operations and best practice, support services and representation. All members are committed to health and safety, skills and integrity and the delivery of the highest standards, professionalism and performance.

The Orkney Construction Training Group organises and co-ordinates training activities within the construction industry as and when required by its member companies, and to liaise with national and local industry bodies in order to promote the training needs of the construction industry.

The group is supported by CITB who, along with the group members, agree annual targets which must be met as a condition of grant funding. This allows OCTG to provide cost effective local training to all members.

Orkney College, which is part of the University of the Highlands and Islands, runs nationally accredited skills training courses for apprentices of the building trade, such as carpentry, joinery and bricklaying. The college also offers courses in traditional building

Energy of Orkney

Orkney is renowned for its wind, wave and tidal energy resources.
World-class test facilities, a wealth of academic and maritime expertise and a growing number of specialist supply chain businesses have helped make Orkney a global centre for renewable energy development

This is a community that continually strives for sustainability, values innovation and embraces efforts to develop a low carbon economy. Indeed, Orkney's entire electricity needs are regularly met from local renewables sources.

Wind turbine power is a well-established technology in the islands, but Orkney is now at the forefront of efforts to develop commercially viable devices to harness wave and tidal energy resources, with the facilities at the European Marine Energy Centre the focus for this pioneering work.

Set up in 2003 and based in Stromness, EMEC is both an open-air laboratory for wave and tidal developers and a global industry standards setter. In addition to its 14 full-scale wave and tidal test berths – now all fully occupied by developers - EMEC operates two smaller-scale wave and tidal sites for device, technique and component testing in less challenging sea conditions. EMEC's team of specialists also provides a range of consultancy and support services, with their expertise much in demand from emerging and planned test sites around the world.

Improving facilities for the emerging renewables industry has been a top priority for local public sector organisations, with Orkney Islands Council investing in major new harbour developments at Hatston near Kirkwall, Lyness, on the island of Hoy, and Stromness. Meanwhile, Highlands and Islands Enterprise has created extensive on-shore facilities for developers at Hatston, with further projects planned for the site and for Lyness.

The Orkney community has been quick to embrace the renewables industry, recognising its enormous economic potential, with increasing numbers of local businesses keen to diversify into the field. Marine energy now supports around 300 jobs in Orkney across a wide range of sectors, from manufacturing and engineering, to marine work, research and consultancy services, with additional posts being created every year.

Orkney Renewable Energy Forum (OREF) promotes all forms of renewable energy and efficiency and facilitates research and development. It also shares information, lobbies on strategic issues affecting renewable energy development and acts as a consultative body. Its full members are based in Orkney and support OREF's aims, but there are also a number of associate members outwith Orkney. Full members and supporters of OREF include renewables companies, service providers, colleges and universities, local development trusts, members of the construction industry and individuals

Fishing Industry in Orkney

Fishing remains an important part of the Orkney economy, with seafood products from the islands famous throughout Britain and beyond for their quality.

Orkney Fisheries Association was established in 1972 when local fishermen, merchants and processors teamed up to fight the threat of joining Europe.

Membership covers vessels in the whitefish, prawn, scallop and creel sectors and until recently there were also pelagic interests. Orkney Fisheries Association is engaged in a wide range of activities to provide a service and representation for its members in the various sectors. It has been the policy of Orkney Fisheries Association that there should be an Orkney voice at all important discussions and the office-bearers and secretary aim to attend most industry meetings and seminars. To complement this, Orkney Fisheries Association rejoined the Scottish

Fishermen's Federation in mid-1999 to promote the Orkney view and enlist the wider representation offered by the Federation.

Other organisations which fishermen and processors may belong to include Seafood Scotland and the Scottish Salmon Producers' Organisation.

There is also a large aquaculture industry in Orkney, with a number of salmon fish farms operated by multi-national companies.

Orkney Food and Drink

Orkney's food and drink producers are enormously proud of what they bring to the marketplace, and they also keen to enhance and promote the famous Orkney brand.

They recognise the need to protect and enhance the islands' reputation for quality and take their role as ambassadors extremely seriously. That's why increasing numbers of local producers are joining membership organisation Orkney Food and Drink (OFD).

OFD's aim is to develop Orkney's food and drink industry through joint representation and promotion at local and national level, spearheading a collective commitment to quality and supporting the efforts of members to maintain the highest of standards across all elements of their business.

Tourism in Orkney

Tourism is one of the most important industries in Orkney, with over 140,000 annual visitors providing a £30 million economic boost to the islands.

Orkney's rich heritage, archaeological treasures, incredible scenery, wildlife, food, drink and crafts are the biggest draws for visitors, along with the islands' many festivals and cultural attractions. The islands are also the top UK destination for cruise liners.

Surveys show that the vast majority of tourists leave Orkney feeling very satisfied with the quality of their experience. That's largely thanks to the local army of hoteliers, guest house and self catering owners, retailers, artisans, chefs, waiting staff and tour guides who work hard to deliver the highest possible standards of service.

Supporting the sector's dedicated workforce is Orkney Tourism Group, which now has more than 400 members. This non-profit making company was founded in 2005 to represent the interests of those involved in Orkney tourism. Its aims include developing tourism by extending the season, increasing the spread of visitors across Orkney, helping operators develop skills and improving transport links.

Tourism businesses also have the support of Visit Scotland which is responsible for the marketing of Orkney outwith the area. It operates a local office and runs staffed visitor centres at the Travel Centre in Kirkwall all year round and at the Ferry Terminal in Stromness during the summer months.

www.ingramcontent.com/pod-product-compliance
Lightning Source LLC
Chambersburg PA
CBHW021103080526
44587CB00010B/364